JERMYN STREET THEATRE

Cancelling Socrates

By Howard Brenton

Performed at Jermyn Street Theatre 2 June – 2 July 2022

Cancelling Socrates
by Howard Brenton

CAST
in order of appearance

EUTHYPHRO	Robert Mountford
SOCRATES	Jonathan Hyde
XANTHIPPE	Hannah Morrish
ASPASIA	Sophie Ward
GAOLER	Robert Mountford

PRODUCTION TEAM

Director	Tom Littler
Set & Costume Designer	Isabella van Braeckel
Lighting Designer	William Reynolds
Sound Co-Designer	Max Pappenheim
Sound Co-Designer	Ali Taie
Assistant Director	Becca Chadder
Movement Associate	Phoebe Hyder
Production Manager	Lucy Mewis-McKerrow
Stage Manager	Lisa Cochrane
Production & Rehearsal Photographer	Steve Gregson
Graphic Designer	Ciaran Walsh
PR	David Burns

Supported by the Director's Circle at Jermyn Street Theatre.
Production supporters: Marit Mohn and Robert Westlake.

Cast

JONATHAN HYDE | SOCRATES

Theatre includes: *Hamlet* (Theatre Royal Windsor); *Gently Down the Stream* (Park Theatre, Olivier Award Nomination); *Hedda Tesman, Rattigan's Nijinsky* (Chichester Festival Theatre); *Frost/Nixon, Julius Caesar* (Crucible Theatre Sheffield); *Travels with My Aunt* (Menier Chocolate Factory); *The King's Speech* (West End/UK tour); *Peter Pan* (London, San Francisco, L.A.); *King Lear, The Seagull* (RSC Stratford/world tour/London); *Antony and Cleopatra, Macbeth, The Merchant of Venice, Romeo and Juliet, Richard II, Richard III, As You Like It, The Roaring Girl, The Swan Down Gloves* (RSC); *Sleep With Me, Jumpers,The Duchess of Malfi, The Real Inspector Hound/The Critic, The Cherry Orchard* (National Theatre); *Macbeth* (Lyceum Theatre Edinburgh); *Antigone* (Old Vic); *The Importance of Being Earnest, Mirandolina* (Olivier Award Nomination); *Chinchilla* (Edinburgh Festival); *The Good-Humoured Ladies, The Country Wife, Figaro, What the Butler Saw, Masquerade, The Seven Deadly Sins, Woyzeck, The Duchess of Malfi, The de Sade Show, The Government Inspector, Sailor Beware, Hamlet, Romeo and Juliet, Coriolanus, Indians, St.Joan of the Stockyards, Camino Real* (Glasgow Citizens Theatre); *The Strange Case of Charles Dexter Ward* (SF Theatre of Liverpool).

Films include: *Titanic, Jumanji, Richie Rich, The Mummy, Caravaggio, Anaconda, The Contract, Breathe, Firstborn, Deadly Advice, Crimson Peak, Hamlet* (tbr).

TV includes: *A Very English Scandal* (BBC); *The Strain* (FX); *Tokyo Trial, Trollhunters* (Netflix); *Isaac Newton, The Last Magician, Shadow of the Noose, Spooks, Joan of Arc, Endeavour, Sherlock Holmes.*

Directed shows: *In and Out of Love with Isobel Buchanan* (Almeida); *In Flanders Fields* (Bath International Music Festival/St Magnus Festival).

ROBERT MOUNTFORD | EUTHYPHRO AND THE GAOLER

For Jermyn Street Theatre: *All's Well That Ends Well* and *The Wind in the Willows* (also Guildford Shakespeare Company), *Vagabonds : My Phil Lynott Odyssey, The Odyssey*.

Theatre includes: *Spike, House and Garden* (UK Theatre Award nomination – Newbury Watermill); *Much Ado About Nothing, Merchant of Venice* (Royal Shakespeare Company); *The Habit of Art, Into The Night, The Haunting of Alice Bowles* (Original Theatre); *The Winter's Tale, Romeo and Juliet* (Guildford Shakespeare Company); *The Omission of the Family Coleman* (Royal Theatre Bath); *Anita & Me* (Birmingham Rep); *Betrayal* (Salisbury Playhouse); *Macbeth, The Tempest, Enemy of the People, Merchant of Venice* (Tara Arts); *The Black Album* (National Theatre).

Television includes: *North Square* (Channel 4); *Holby City, EastEnders, Silent Witness, Torn, One Night, Casualty, Michael Wood's History of India, Reverse Psychology* (BBC); *London's Burning* (London Weekend Television); *A&E* (Granada).

His solo show – *Vagabonds – My Phil Lynott Odyssey* has played to sell-out audiences in Edinburgh, Dublin & London, he regularly appears for *Read not Dead* at Shakespeare's Globe and has been a guest for acclaimed Shakespeare Impro Group The School of Night.

HANNAH MORRISH | XANTHIPPE

For Jermyn Street Theatre: *All's Well That Ends Well* (also Guildford Shakespeare Company), *Hole, The Odyssey.*

Theatre includes: *Antony and Cleopatra* (National Theatre)*; Coriolanus, Titus Andronicus, Julius Caesar* (Royal Shakespeare Company); *Arms and the Man* (Watford Palace Theatre); *Flowering Cherry* (Finborough); *Goodnight Children Everywhere, Madness in Valencia, Paradise Lost, The Cherry Orchard, Rose Bernd, Pygmalion* (Drama Centre); *A Little Hotel on the Side* (Theatre Royal Bath).

Hannah received a commendation in the Ian Charleson Awards 2017 for playing Lavinia in *Titus Andronicus* (Royal Shakespeare Company) and was awarded second place in the Ian Charleson Awards 2018 for playing Octavia in *Antony and Cleopatra* (National Theatre).

Film includes: *Ceres* (Short, Kusini Productions); *Magpie* (Paul Cook Film); *Nell and Pauline* (Short)*; No More Kings* (Short); *Arcade* (Short, BM Productions/BFI).

Television includes: *Father Brown, Call the Midwife* (BBC).

SOPHIE WARD | ASPASIA

For Jermyn Street Theatre: *Flowers of the Forest.*

Theatre credits include: *The Exorcist, A Judgement In Stone, Go Back for Murder, The Grass is Greener* (Bill Kenwright Ltd); *Dark Sublime* (Trafalgar Studios); *Paradise Circus* (Playground Theatre); *Mount Vernon* (King's Head Theatre/Hudson La/Vindicate Company); *But It Still Goes On* (Finborough Theatre); *Brave New World* (Royal & Derngate); *Private Lives* (Carpe); *One Flew Over the Cuckoo's Nest* (Nimax Tour); *An Ideal Husband* (Clwyd Theatre); *Nothing* (59e59 New York), *Electricity* (West Yorkshire Playhouse); *Venice Preserved, The Robbers, Hamlet, Don Carlos, Private Lives, The Milk Train* and *Flare Path* (Glasgow Citizens Theatre); *Semi-Monde* (Lyric Theatre); *Les Liaisons Dangereuses* (UK tour); *The Turn of the Screw* (Belgrade Theatre).

Television includes: *Picture Perfect Royal Christmas* (Free Dolphin Productions); *The Moonstone* (BBC/King Bert Productions); *Doctors, Casualty,Holby City, New Tricks, The Inspector Lynley Mysteries, Land Girls Series 1-3, Rhona, A Dark Adapted Eye, Screenplay, A Very British Scandal, Strike* (BBC); *Secret State* (Company Pictures); *Hustle* (AMC); *Law & Order: UK* (BBC America/Kudos); *Lewis* (Granada Media); *Heartbeat* (Granada Television); *Dinotopia* (ABC Productions); *Peak Practice* (Central Independent Television); *Welcome To Orty-Fou* (Carlton Television); *Crusade* (Babylon Productions/TNT); *The Nanny* (CBS); *A Village Affair* (Carlton Television); *Chille*r (Yorkshire Television), *Macgyver: Lost Treasure of Atlantis* (Gekko Film Corp/ABC); *Class Of '61* (Amblin Entertainment); *Strauss Dynasty* (ECA Partners/Beta Film); *Agatha Raisin* (Sky).

Her film credits include; *Swiperight, Jane Eyre, Book of Blood, Out of Bounds, Nobody Knows Anything, Crime & Punishment, Bela Donna, Taking Liberty, Wuthering Heights, Waxwork II: Lost In Time, A Demon in My View, The Monk, Una Vita Scellerata, Young Toscanini, A Summer Story, Little Dorrit, Aria, Return To Oz, The Hunger, The Lords of Discipline, The Haunting of Julia* and *The Copter Kids.*

Creative Team

HOWARD BRENTON | WRITER

Howard Brenton was born in 1942. He began to write for the emerging fringe theatre in the late 1960s, the Royal Court made him Writer-in-Residence in 1973 and he went on to write for many theatres, among them the Royal Shakespeare Company, National Theatre, Shakespeare's Globe and Hampstead Theatre. His plays include *The Romans In Britain* (1980), *Bloody Poetry* (1983) and *Pravda* (1985, written with David Hare). *Thirteenth Night* was performed by the Royal Shakespeare Company in 1981. Plays this century include *Paul* (2005), *Never So Good* (2008) and a version of Büchner's *Danton's Death* (2010) at the National Theatre; *In Extremis* (2008), *Anne Boleyn* (2010) and *Doctor Scroggy's War* (2014) at Shakespeare's Globe; *55 Days* (2012), T*he Arrest of Ai Weiwei* (2013), *Drawing The Line* (2013) and *Lawrence After Arabia* (2016) at Hampstead Theatre and *The Shadow Factory* (2018) at Southampton's Nuffield Theatre. For Jermyn Street Theatre, Tom Littler asked Brenton to explore the work of August Strindberg and he wrote *The Blinding Light* (2017), about Strindberg's 'Inferno' crisis, and versions of *Miss Julie* (2017) and *Creditors* (2019).

TOM LITTLER | DIRECTOR

For Jermyn Street Theatre: *The Tempest, 15 Heroines* (also Digital Theatre), *All's Well That Ends Well* (also Guildford Shakespeare Company), *For Services Rendered, Pictures of Dorian Gray* (also Stephen Joseph Theatre/Creation), *Tonight at 8.30, Miss Julie* and *Creditors* (also Theatre by the Lake),*The Blinding Light, First Episode, The Living Room, Bloody Poetry, Anyone Can Whistle, Saturday Night* (also West End).

Theatre includes: *Hamlet, She Stoops to Conquer, Love's Labour's Lost, Much Ado About Nothing, Twelfth Night, The Wind in the Willows* (Guildford Shakespeare Company); *Dear Uncle, Single Spies* (Theatre by the Lake); *Dances of Death* (Gate); *Good Grief* (Theatre Royal Bath/UK tour); *Romeo and Juliet, Measure for Measure* (Cambridge Arts); *As You Like It* (Creation); *Cabaret* (Frankfurt/Munich); *Switzerland, Jekyll and Hyde, The Glass Menagerie, Other Desert Cities, The Picture of Dorian Gray, Strangers on a Train* (Frankfurt); *Absurd Person Singular* (Sonning and UK tours); *Martine, Jingo* (Finborough); *Antigone* (Southwark Playhouse); *Shiverman, Madagascar* (Theatre503); *Murder in the Cathedral* (Christ Church Cathedral); *A Little Night Music* (Budapest).

Tom is Artistic Director and Executive Producer at Jermyn Street Theatre, where he won the 2022 OffWestEnd Award for Best Artistic Director. He was previously Associate Director at Theatre503, founder and Artistic Director of Primavera, and Associate Director of the Peter Hall Company. He trained as associate director to Peter Hall and Trevor Nunn, among many others. Tom has been nominated eight times for the OffWestEnd Best Director Award. He lives in Cambridge, where he teaches English Literature at the university.

ISABELLA VAN BRAECKEL | DESIGNER

For Jermyn Street Theatre: *The Dog Walker*.

Theatre includes: *The Dwarfs* (White Bear); *Gatsby* (Southwark Playhouse); *Liminal* (King's Head); *Dual* (VAULT Festival); *Piloten, Polarörnen, Midnattståget till Marrakech* (Teateri, Jönköping); *The Hunchback of Notre Dame* (St Paul's Church); *When The Birds Come, This is Living* (Edinburgh Fringe); *Hell Yes I'm Tough Enough* (Park 90); *The Travelling Companion* (Cadogan Hall/Saffron Hall); *A Funny Thing Happened [...], Finishing the Picture, Into the Numbers* (Finborough); *Macbeth* (UK/Ireland tour); *Red INK* (tour/Leicester Curve/Southbank Centre); *Blush of Dogs* (Tabard Theatre).

Associate Design: *Rice* (UK tour); *Burgerz* (Hackney Showroom/Traverse/tour); *The Boys in the Band* (Park 200/Vaudeville/tour); *Eclipsed* (Gate Theatre).

Upcoming: *Secret Cinema Presents: Dirty Dancing* (Secret Cinema); *The Lesson* (Southwark Playhouse); *The Ring Cycle* (Regent Opera).

Isabella is a Designer for Performance, specialising in New Writing, Opera and Dance across Fringe Theatre and in the West End. She is a Jerwood Young Designer and was featured in the UK Exhibit 'Staging Spaces' at the Prague Quadrennial and V&A.

WILLIAM REYNOLDS | LIGHTING DESIGNER

For Jermyn Street Theatre: *The Tempest, Pictures of Dorian Gray* (also Stephen Joseph Theatre/Creation), *Parents' Evening, Stitchers, The Blinding Light, Bloody Poetry, Saturday Night* (also Theatre Royal Windsor & Arts Theatre).

Design includes: *Madam Butterfly* (OperaUpClose); *The Process* (Bunker Theatre); *In the Willows* (Exeter Northcott & UK tour); *Smoke & Mirrors* (Aurora Orchestra); *Trying It On* (Royal Shakespeare Company, Royal Court & UK tour); *Sonnet Walks* (Globe Theatre); *Little Mermaid* (Theatre by the Lake & UK tour); *Jungle Book* (London Wonderground & international tour); *Blown Away* (Lyric Hammersmith & international tour); *Radiant Vermin* (Soho Theatre & Brits Off Broadway),

Video design includes: *Prima Donna* (Sadler's Wells), *The Gambler* (Royal Opera House).

William is Artistic Director of Metta Theatre and recently Artist-in-Residence at the V&A Museum. Alongside his design work, William is a Creative Climate Leader and offers Environmental Sustainability consultancy to projects, individuals and organisations across the arts industry, supporting use of the Theatre Green Book and in developing and implementing bespoke green policies and action plans.

MAX PAPPENHEIM | SOUND CO-DESIGNER

For Jermyn Street Theatre: *Two Horsemen, The Tempest, The Blinding Light, Miss Julie* and *Creditors* (also Theatre by the Lake), *15 Heroines* (also Digital Theatre).

Theatre includes: *The Night of the Iguana, Cruise* (West End); *The Way of the World, Assembly* (Donmar Warehouse); *The Children* (Royal Court/ Broadway); *Ophelias Zimmer* (Schaubühne, Berlin/Royal Court); *The Fever Syndrome, Labyrinth* (Hampstead); *Old Bridge* (Bush Theatre; OffWestEnd Award for Sound Design); *The Homecoming, My Cousin Rachel* (Theatre Royal Bath/national tour); *Crooked Dances* (RSC); *Macbeth* (Chichester); *One Night in Miami* (Nottingham Playhouse); *Hogarth's Progress* (Rose Theatre Kingston); *Waiting for Godot* (Sheffield Crucible); *The Ridiculous Darkness* (Gate Theatre); *Amsterdam, Blue/Heart, The Distance* (Orange Tree); *The Gaul* (Hull Truck); *Jane Wenham* (Out of Joint); *CommonWealth* (Almeida); *Creve Coeur* (Print Room); *Cuzco, Wink* (Theatre503); *Switzerland, The Glass Menagerie* (English Theatre, Frankfurt); *Yellowfin* (Southwark Playhouse); *Martine* (Finborough); *A Splinter of Ice, Being Mr Wickham* (Original Theatre).

Online includes: *The System, Barnes' People* (Original Theatre).

Opera includes: *Miranda* (Opéra Comique, Paris); *Hansel and Gretel* (BYO/Opera Holland Park); *Bluebeard's Castle* (Theatre of Sound); *Scraww* (Trebah Gardens); *Vixen* (Vaults/international tour).

Radio includes: *Home Front* (BBC Radio 4).

Associate Artist of The Faction and Silent Opera.

ALI TAIE | SOUND CO-DESIGNER

For Jermyn Street Theatre: *Assault with a Deadly Weapon* (Opsis, Footprints Festival), *15 Heroines* (as Assistant). Ali was a 2020/21 Creative Associate.

Theatre includes: *Spindrift* (Curious Directive); *The Woods* (Southwark Playhouse); *Regeneration* (Jack Studio Theatre); *Body* (Opsis); *Wait 'Til The End* (The Pappy Show); *4.48 Psychosis* (Opsis).

Theatre includes (as Associate): "*Daddy*" (Almeida Theatre).

Music includes: *brkbts4brxt* – korghett ft. DJ Enerate; *Clockwork EP* – Thalash.

Ali is currently studying Theatre Sound at the Royal Central School of Speech and Drama.

BECCA CHADDER | ASSISTANT DIRECTOR

Theatre includes (as assistant director): *The Ballad of Maria Marten* (Eastern Angles); *Cabildo* (Wilton's Music Hall); *START* (Mountview Academy of Theatre Arts).

As Writer/Director: *La Voisin* (London Horror Fest); *Number, Please.* (Edinburgh Fringe, tour).

As Writer: *The Girl of Ink and Stars by Kiran Millwood Hargrave* (The Watermill Theatre Youth Ensemble).

Becca recently graduated with an MA in Theatre Directing from Mountview Academy of Theatre Arts and is currently a Playwright in Residence at The Watermill Theatre. She is a 2022/23 Creative Associate at Jermyn Street Theatre, where she will soon be directing *The Poison Belt*.

LISA COCHRANE | STAGE MANAGER

For Jermyn Street Theatre: *This Beautiful Future, 15 Heroines, For Services Rendered, Miss Julie, Creditors, About Leo, The Play about My Dad, Tonight at 8.30, All Our Children.*

Theatre credits as Deputy Stage Manager include: *Hamlet, Macbeth* (Guildford Shakespeare Company); *The Offing* (Stephen Joseph Theatre/ Live); *King Lear* (Grange Festival Opera); *Emilia* (Mountview); *Vienna '34 – Munich '38* (Theatre Royal Bath); *Peter Pan, Dick Whittington, Snow White and the Seven Dwarfs* (Swan Theatre, High Wycombe).

As Company Stage Manager on book: *Habibti Driver* (Bolton Octagon) *Songs For Nobodies* (Olivier Award nominated, Ambassadors Theatre); *The Hunting of the Snark* (Queen Elizabeth Hall).

As Stage Manager on book: *Honour* (Park Theatre); *Fog Everywhere* (Camden People's Theatre); *Disco Pigs* (Trafalgar Studios); *Acedian Pirates* (Theatre503); *My Mother Said I Never Should* (The Other Palace); *Land of Our Fathers* (Trafalgar Studios/UK tour/ Found111).

JERMYN STREET THEATRE

Honorary Patron
HRH Princess
Michael of Kent

Patron
Sir Michael Gambon

Artistic Director & Executive Producer
Tom Littler

Executive Director
Penny Horner

Carne Deputy Director
Ebenezer Bamgboye*

Resident Producer
David Doyle

Production Manager
Lucy Mewis-McKerrow

Marketing Officer
Darcy Dobson

Graphic Designer
Ciaran Walsh

PR
David Burns

Production Assistant
Kayleigh Hunt

Building Manager
Jon Wadey

Artistic Associates
Stella Powell-Jones
Natasha Rickman

Associate Designer
Louie Whitemore

Interns
Ryan Abrams
Lola Oniya
Elvira Parr

Business Development
Chris Parkinson

In-House Technical Staff
David Harvey
Steve Lowe

Box Office Manager
Kayleigh Hunt

FOH Duty Managers
Christina Gazelidis
Adam Ishaq
Adam Lilley
Mark Magill
Alex Pearson
Rohan Perumatantri
Grace Wessels

Day Staff
Laura Jury-Hyde
Scarlett Stitt

Bar Team
Mandy Berger
Aren Johnston

Web Design
Robin Powell / Ideasfor

Web Development
Robert Iles / Dynamic Listing

*The Carne Deputy Director position is supported by Philip and Christine Carne.

Creative Associates
Becca Chadder
Millie Gaston
Catja Hamilton
Phoebe Hyder
maatin
Caitlin Mawhinney
Jo Walker
Imy Wyatt Corner

Creative Associate Company
Definitely Fine

With thanks to Leslie Macleod-Miller for his sponsorship of the bar at Jermyn Street Theatre - the **Sandra Macleod-Miller Mini Bar**.

Jermyn Street Theatre staff salaries are supported by the **Backstage Trust**.

The Creative Associates programme and Footprints Festival are supported by:
Philip and Christine Carne
The Fenton Arts Trust
The Garrick Charitable Trust
The Harold Hyam Wingate Foundation
Everyone who contributed to our Christmas Auction.

Individual Creative Associates sponsored by **Jocelyn Abbey**, **Judith Johnstone** and **Peter Wilson**.

---

a small theatre with big stories

James Sheldon and Charlotte Hamblin in Miss Julie, 2019. Photo by Keith Pattison.

WHO WE ARE

Jermyn Street Theatre is a unique theatre in the heart of the West End: a home to remarkable artists and plays, performed in the most intimate and welcoming of surroundings. World-class, household-name playwrights, directors and actors work here alongside people just taking their first steps in professional theatre. It is a crucible for multigenerational talent.

The programme includes outstanding new plays, rare revivals, new versions of European classics, and high-quality musicals, alongside one-off musical and literary events. We collaborate with theatres across the world, and our productions have transferred to the West End and Broadway. Recently, our pioneering online work and theatre-on-film has been enjoyed across the world.

A registered charity No. 1186940, Jermyn Street Theatre was founded in 1994 with no core funding from government or the Arts Council. Since then, the theatre has survived and thrived thanks to a mixture of earned income from box office sales and the generous support of individual patrons and trusts and foundations. In 2017, we became a producing theatre, the smallest in London's West End. Around 60% of our income comes from box office sales, and the rest in charitable support and private funding.

“ Unerringly directed ... no one in this tiny theatre dared breathe. ”

The Observer

THE NUMBERS

Nearly **50,000** audience members have come to see our shows in our first five years as a producing theatre.

Produced **40** world premiere shows.

30 new plays have been published in the UK after starting here.

In 2020, our digital content on YouTube was viewed **117,896** times.

★★★★★

“An unexpected treat of the highest order.”

The Evening Standard

OVER THE YEARS

1930s During the 1930s, the basement of 16b Jermyn Street was home to the glamorous Monseigneur Restaurant and Club.

early 1990s

1994 The staff changing rooms were transformed into a theatre by Howard Jameson and Penny Horner (who continue to serve as Chair of the Board and Executive Director today) in the early 1990s and Jermyn Street Theatre staged its first production in August 1994.

1995 Neil Marcus became the first Artistic Director in 1995 and secured Lottery funding for the venue; producer Chris Grady also made a major contribution to the theatre's development.

late 1990s In 1995, HRH Princess Michael of Kent became the theatre's Patron and David Babani, subsequently the Artistic Director of the Menier Chocolate Factory, took over as Artistic Director until 2001. Later Artistic Directors included Gene David Kirk and Anthony Biggs.

2012 The theatre won the Stage Award for Fringe Theatre of the Year.

2017 Tom Littler restructured the theatre to become a full-time producing house.

2020 Our audiences and supporters helped us survive the damaging impacts of the Covid-19 lockdowns and we were able to produce a season of largely digital work, including the award-winning *15 Heroines* with Digital Theatre +.

2021 We won the Stage Award for Fringe Theatre of the Year for a second time. Artistic Director Tom Littler and Executive Director Penny Horner were recognised in The Stage 100.

2022 We won a Critics' Circle Award for *Exceptional Theatre-Making During Lockdown* and an OffWestEnd Award for our Artistic Director.

(Clockwise from top) David Threlfall in Beckett Triple Bill, 2020. Photo by Robert Workman; Sinead Cusack in Stitchers, 2018. Photo by Robert Workman.

support us

"I recently became a Patron of Jermyn Street Theatre, as I believe passionately in the work it is doing. It would be wonderful if you could contribute."
Sir Michael Gambon

We have four tiers of Friends with names inspired by *The Tempest*. Please consider joining our Friends to support a small, independent charity that needs your help.

Lifeboat Friends

(£4.16 to £12.42 a month)

Our **Lifeboat Friends** are the heart of Jermyn Street Theatre. Their support keeps us going. Rewards include priority booking to ensure they can get the best seats in the house.

The Ariel Club

(£12.43 to £41 a month)

Members of the **Ariel Club** enjoy exclusive access to the theatre and our team. As well as the priority booking and Friends Nights enjoyed by Lifeboat Friends, **Ariel Club** members also enjoy a range of other benefits.

The Miranda Club

(£42 to £249 a month)

Members of the **Miranda Club** enjoy all the benefits of the Ariel Club, and they enjoy a closer relationship with the theatre.

The Director's Circle

(From £250 a month)

The Director's Circle is an exclusive inner circle of our biggest donors. They are invited to every press night and enjoy regular informal contact with our Artistic Director and team. They are the first to hear our plans and often act as a valuable sounding board. We are proud to call them our friends.

We only have 70 seats which makes attending our theatre a magical experience but even if we sell every seat, we still need to raise more funds. **Michael Gambon** (our new Honorary Patron), **Sinead Cusack, Richard Griffiths, David Warner, Joely Richardson, Danny Lee Wynter, Rosalie Craig, Trevor Nunn, Adjoa Andoh, David Suchet, Tuppence Middleton, Martina Laird, Gemma Whelan, Eileen Atkins, Jimmy Akingbola** and many more have starred at the theatre.

But even more importantly, hundreds of young actors and writers have started out here.

If you think you could help support our theatre, then please visit www.jermynstreettheatre.co.uk/friends/

Jermyn Street Theatre is a Registered Charity No. 1186940. 60% of our income comes from box office sales and the remaining 40% comes from charitable donations. That means we need your help.

our friends

The Ariel Club

Richard Alexander
David Barnard
Martin Bishop
Katie Bradford
Nigel Britten
Christopher Brown
Donald Campbell
James Carroll
Ted Craig
Jeanette Culver
Valerie Dias
Robyn Durie
Shomit Dutta
Maureen Elton
Anthony Gabriel
Carol Gallagher
Roger Gaynham
Paul Guinery
Diana Halfnight
Julie Harries
Andrew Hughes
Margaret Karliner
David Lanch
Keith Macdonald
Vivien Macmillan-Smith
Nicky Oliver
Kate & John Peck
Adrian Platt
A J P Powell
Oliver Prenn
Martin Sanderson
Nicholas Sansom
Andrew WG Savage
Nigel Silby
Bernard Silverman
Anthony Skyrme
Philip Somervail
Robert Swift
Paul Taylor
Gary Trimby
Kevin Tuffnell
Ian Williams
Marie Winckler
John Wise

The Miranda Club

Anthony Ashplant
Derek Baum
Geraldine Baxter
Gyles Brandreth
Anthony Cardew
Tim Cribb
Sylvia de Bertodano
Anne Dunlop
Nora Franglen
Pirjo Gardiner
Mary Godwin
Louise Greenberg
Ros Haigh
Phyllis Huvos
Frank Irish
Marta Kinally
Yvonne Koenig
Hilary Lemaire
Jane Mennie
Charles Paine
John Pearson
Iain Reid
Martin Shenfield
Carol Shephard-Blandy
Jenny Sheridan
Brian Smith
Dana-Leigh Strauss
Mark Tantam
Esme Tyers
Jatinder Verma

Director's Circle

Anonymous
Michael & Gianni Alen-Buckley
Judith Burnley
Philip & Christine Carne
Jocelyn Abbey & Tom Carney
Colin Clark RIP
Lynette & Robert Craig
Flora Fraser
Charles Glanville & James Hogan
Crawford & Mary Harris
Judith Johnstone
Ros & Duncan McMillan
Leslie Macleod-Miller
James Simon
Marjorie Simonds-Gooding
Fiona Stone
Peter Soros & Electra Toub
Melanie Vere Nicoll
Robert Westlake & Marit Mohn

The City and the Social Gadfly

If Athens at the turn of the 4th Century BC feels like a familiar place – democracy, law courts, frenetic international trade, flourishing arts (especially theatre) and lots of wine – it was also terrifyingly alien.

Yes, there was democracy; but Greek and especially Athenian democracy was radical. (Modern 'democracies' would never pass as such to the Greeks; Westminster might at best be called 'representative oligarchy', with local authorities vaguely akin to the division into tribes.) Endless debating and endless voting dominated politics, with a complex set of forums and committees ranging from the Council of 500 to the General Assembly, which needed at least 6000 to attend. Referendum piled up on referendum. The democratic apparatus became so clogged that turnout nosedived; eventually the city had to pay voters to show up. Not that it occurred to the Athenians to let women participate: only native male adult citizens were allowed to vote, or address their fellow decision-makers. Perhaps the most regular decision of this great assembly was to go to war – as lamented by the city's women in one particularly biting Athenian comedy, *Lysistrata*. (The women find a novel remedy to the situation: they withhold sex from their partners until the men relent and seek peace.)

Athens grew into a 'city of words'. Gaining power meant winning votes, and winning votes meant oratory. The statesmen whose names have come to us – Pericles, Alcibiades, Demosthenes – were master strategists in politics and in war, but their strategies might have come to nothing without the rhetoric to back them up. Every institution of government needed coaxing, cajoling and at times terrorising into submission. Persuasion was everything. Words were an industry, too: professional speech-writers thrived, especially in the law courts. The parties spoke for themselves, but with no guarantee that the words were their own. Speech was necessarily free; but with that freedom came responsibility. Apart from the risk of prosecution for dangerous beliefs, Athens had ostracism, by which the citizens could vote to exile anyone sufficiently unpopular.

Meanwhile the arts were essential to life, both personal and civic, and were heavily subsidised by the state; but the arts were also heavily religious and ritualised. Even theatre had grown out of choral dances, and the mythological subject-matter routinely featured gruesome deaths, appalling dilemmas, and labyrinthine plots where a god might save (or ruin) the day on a whim. Religious festivals acted as a kind of social pressure-valve, ranging from the idiosyncratic to the downright bizarre. At the secretive Thesmophoria, for example, married women withdrew on a camping trip to sacrifice to the goddess Demeter; men were utterly forbidden to attend or know of the religious mysteries. Men, for their part, would regularly socialise at a highly ritualised drinking-and-dining party known as a symposium whose formal structure endured for centuries – even as far, some have suggested, as the Last Supper.

There was not yet any such country as Greece; Athens was just one of many city-states, democratic and otherwise. Underpinning the Greek identity was a shared language, and one particular shared cultural asset: the poems of Homer. Homer was familiar to everyone, in intimate detail. Those lucky enough to have a formal education would have memorised much of the *Iliad* and *Odyssey*; everyone else would recognise a Homer reference in an instant. Imagine Shakespeare's cultural heft, but turbo-charged to absolute supremacy.

The streets, crammed and colourful (the purity of white marble was never Greek; temples and statues alike were brightly painted) heaved with trade, and – critically for a pre-literate society – with symbols. Perhaps most alien to us would be the ubiquitous Herms: weirdly stylised statues, a head atop a column, frequently with prominent male genitals beneath, putting sexuality and fertility in full sight. When the Herms were vandalised one night shortly before a critical military expedition, the effect on public optimism was devastating.

Because above all, despite democratic freedom, the rule of law, and the vast scope of international trade and multiculturalism (the Greeks' own alphabet was pinched from the Phoenicians; iconic temple architecture borrows heavily from Egyptian styles, and philosophy itself first arose in Ionia in the Eastern Mediterranean before making its home in Athens), Greek society remained utterly religious. Most notably, the Greeks lived in thrall to the Oracles. Their cryptic prophecies had ultimate authority. (The Delphic Oracle was particularly important – and notorious for its slippery ways. King Croesus of Lydia was told 'if you make war on the Persians, you shall destroy a mighty empire.' Thinking he had oracular approval, he set off for Persia – but the empire he destroyed turned out to be his own.)

The conservativism of religion might help explain the limitations of democracy. Most jarringly, this was a society that owned slaves. Slaves almost certainly outnumbered citizens; three or four enslaved workers per household would be quite normal. There was a huge range of experience, from that of a prisoner of war condemned to work in a mine or building roads as a slave of the state, to a household slave who might live, eat, and travel with their owners, and even deputise for them on business. At the latter end of the scale a slave might eventually buy their own freedom and even, as occasionally documented, end up wealthier than their former masters. Artistic depictions of slaves suggest that such contradictions exercised the Greeks' conscience and social anxieties. When in Aristophanes' comedy *Frogs* the god Dionysus and his cunning slave Xanthias repeatedly swap costumes to get each other in and out of trouble, we see signs of a culture wondering whether the old way is still the best way.

All this made a complex backdrop to the rise of a new type of thinker: philosophers. Initially, these critical thinkers theorised at first about the nature of the universe, chemical elements and states of matter. In time, the focus shifted towards ethics and the nature of reason. Such questions began to break free from the religious arena; but these early 'pre-Socratic' philosophers were not atheists.

Neither, it seems, was Socrates (c.470–399 BCE). He left no writings of his own; everything we think we know is through the pens of his pupils Plato and Xenophon, and others with various axes to grind. He may have been taught by Aspasia, wife of the statesman Pericles and an influential thinker; she appears in a number of Plato's writings. He married twice; portrayals of Xanthippe were not kind, but again we hear nothing from Socrates himself. Living a life free of material pleasures (although inheriting sufficiently to have few financial concerns) he lived as the archetypal unworldly thinker. That is, apart from his military service, which was apparently distinguished. With no professional army, Athens called up even its philosophers.

Evidently Socrates's primary concern was working out how close a human life can reach towards virtue, or 'that which is good'. Along the way he advanced the study of reason, consciousness, knowledge. Plato, describing Socrates not in dry essays but in lively dialogues laid out as playscripts, shows him teaching even the most stubborn acquaintances that their knowledge is not as certain as they think. When they protest, he insists that he himself knows nothing: infuriating and disarming in equal measure! Small wonder that his character became a figure of fun, even appearing (twisted into a teacher of rhetorical tricks) in Aristophanes' comedy ***Clouds***.

How, then, did Socrates end up on trial, at risk of his life? It is a great paradox: a rational, free thinker in a rational, democratic society, on the wrong end of the legal system, when his only action was to ask questions. But again, the picture is complex. War with the Persian empire; the Peloponnesian War with other Greek states; the temporary suspension of democracy and rule of the Thirty Tyrants in 404 BCE: Athens was rarely out of turmoil. 'The unexamined life is not worth living', Socrates taught; but perhaps this was one self-proclaimed 'social gadfly' the Athenians did not need?

Max Pappenheim

Max Pappenheim studied Classics and Historical Linguistics at the University of Cambridge, and is a teacher and examiner of Ancient Greek, Latin and Classical Civilisation.

CANCELLING SOCRATES

Howard Brenton

Characters

SOCRATES, *seventy*
EUTHYPHRO, *thirty-five*
ASPASIA, *seventy*
XANTHIPPE, *thirty*
GAOLER, *thirty-five*
A DAEMON

Euthyphro doubles up as the Gaoler, Xanthippe as a Daemon

Place

Athens.

Time

April to May, 399 BC.

This text went to press before the end of rehearsals and so may differ slightly from the play as performed.

Scene One: The Funnel Web

The Agora, Athens. Late April, 399 BC.

Crowded.

EUTHYPHRO, *smoothed, respectably dressed, his hair well cut and oiled. He is relaxed, smiling and greeting people.*

EUTHYPHRO. Yes yes, thank you for asking, he's quite recovered, my wife too, thank you –

Turns and listens to someone else.

Absolutely, looking forward to it –

Listens, smiling, then shares laughter.

Oh, the flute player with the blue – she will? Well – more water with my wine this time, I think –

Laughter. Then someone of superior rank addresses him. He adopts serious concern.

But I sent a messenger to you this morning, perhaps he didn't – anyway, it is the best of news, my ship's been sighted, it'll be at Piraeus tomorrow. (*Listens respectfully.*) Yes, reported to look fully laden. (*Listens.*) Yes, sir, the future, certainly.

He pulls himself erect, very satisfied with these encounters.

(*Aside.*) Public face, public space. To see to be seen. Normally, as if in normal times. What is civilisation? The art of living in cities. The cultivation of the good between us. And I love it so, as do we all. It is a duty to see and to be seen. After what we have been through – plague, war, the – unfortunate politics – to bounce back to normal. And do what is right by the gods. The one thing we can all agree on, surely, is that religious duty is all.

Enter SOCRATES. *He has straggly grey hair, is reputably dressed and is barefoot. He radiates energy.*

EUTHYPHRO *has not seen him.*

SOCRATES. Euthyphro, my friend!

EUTHYPHRO. Oh no, no, no, please not, no –

SOCRATES. Is all well?

EUTHYPHRO (*aside*). This is the nightmare of public places, meeting the oddballs in one's clan.

He turns, a beamingly false smile.

Socrates!

SOCRATES. My dear, so good to see you, and looking so sleek.

EUTHYPHRO. And you, Socrates, looking so –

SOCRATES. – Still alive?

EUTHYPHRO. Absolutely!

SOCRATES. But I could be a corpse walking around, any signs of life a rhetorical trick.

EUTHYPHRO. Ha! – No, you're one of the fittest men I know, despite your –

A gesture meaning 'the way you dress'. SOCRATES *shoots up a finger.*

SOCRATES. Interesting! Can we prove we are alive? And not, say, ghosts in Hades, doomed to re-enact memories of life? Not alive at all, merely talking to ourselves?

EUTHYPHRO. Socrates, forgive me, at this moment I can't get into a philosophical, er –

SOCRATES. Tangle? No, no, I twitch, I twitch.

SOCRATES *claps his hands, laughs and they embrace.*

I heard your little son was sick?

EUTHYPHRO. It was just a chest infection not the – . His mother had a touch of it too, but they are both well.

SOCRATES. Great to hear it. May youth forever bloom.

EUTHYPHRO. Ha! Yes.

SOCRATES *is beaming at him.*

(*Aside.*) Oh gods, gods –

But he beams back.

SOCRATES. So why are you outside the magistrates' court, nothing serious I hope, on this beautiful day?

EUTHYPHRO. I have come to make a charge of murder.

SOCRATES. My dear! Against whom?

EUTHYPHRO. My father.

SOCRATES *is shocked.*

SOCRATES. You are accusing your own father of murder?

EUTHYPHRO. It's very painful. But to do justice is a religious duty. And justice lies with the gods, who would dispute that?

SOCRATES. No one in their senses. But – whom did your father kill? A relative – it must be, you wouldn't prosecute him for killing a stranger.

EUTHYPHRO. Why should it make a difference if he's killed a relative or a stranger?

SOCRATES. Only human nature – never mind. But I'm agog, tell, tell!

EUTHYPHRO. I had a steward, he visited my father's estate on Naxos. A good administrator, knew how to crack the whip, but – he got drunk, flew into a rage and killed one of my father's slaves. My father had my steward beaten up, bound and thrown in a ditch.

SOCRATES. Ah. And called for the local justices?

EUTHYPHRO. No, he called for a priest to come and give religious advice.

SOCRATES. Religious advice?

EUTHYPHRO. Yes. Do the gods see slaves as being human?

SOCRATES. That is a question.

EUTHYPHRO. My father wanted to be told 'yes', then he could prosecute my steward.

SOCRATES. I can see that.

EUTHYPHRO. Unfortunately the priest didn't arrive until the morning. My man was left in the ditch and died during the night.

SOCRATES. That was callous of your father.

EUTHYPHRO. More than callous, murderous.

SOCRATES. What's your family say about all this?

EUTHYPHRO. Well, they say at worst he murdered a murderer, but it was an accident and anyway my man deserved it. I'm afraid they are being very abusive, they call me a sanctimonious prick. Among other things.

SOCRATES (*musing*). Sanctimonious – pretending to be very holy or pious, affecting sanctity or righteousness. But if you *are* pious, if you are acting with sanctity, if you are righteous – they're just calling you names. Maybe it should be an admirable thing, to be sanctimonious.

EUTHYPHRO. You're right! Piety is easily slandered.

SOCRATES. But, Euthyphro – accusing your own father?

EUTHYPHRO. Justice –

SOCRATES. – is a religious duty and lies with the gods, yes, you've said. I see you're much wiser than I in these matters, so, my friend, teach me. Justice is a matter of what is holy and unholy?

EUTHYPHRO. As every citizen knows, surely.

SOCRATES. Mm. (*A beat.*) The pious and the impious.

SOCRATES *pauses for a moment, thinking.*

The holy and the unholy, what would you say they are?

EUTHYPHRO. Well, I'd say what I'm doing now, prosecuting a wrongdoer, that's holy. And not to do so – that would be unholy. That is the law! It is not unholy to turn on your father, if he has done wrong. After all Zeus put his father Chronos in shackles. And Chronos castrated his father Uranus for eating his children.

SOCRATES. Yes, a long line of fathers doing the right thing. I don't know, when people tell me these stories about the gods, I get itchy. I can't bring myself to believe them. But, as a religious man, you believe the stories?

EUTHYPHRO. Of course. They are the acts of the gods.

SOCRATES. And, of course, the gods are holy.

EUTHYPHRO. Obviously, they are the gods –

SOCRATES. And it's obvious too that they love what is holy.

EUTHYPHRO. Yes –

SOCRATES. So – (*He pauses.*) Is what is holy loved by the gods because it is holy, or is it holy because it is loved by the gods?

Sudden caution from EUTHYPHRO. *Dangerous ground.*

EUTHYPHRO. I – that's too twisty for me, I don't follow –

SOCRATES. Yes, forgive me, my dear, there's a tangle here, a bit of a ball of string that's got knotted up and we philosophers do love knots. It's the problem of what is a quality in a thing or action.

EUTHYPHRO. Is it?

SOCRATES. Bear with me. (*A beat.*) Right! Go! When a thing is carried – when a cup of wine, say, is carried across a room – the cup has the innate quality of carriedness.

EUTHYPHRO. Yeeeees –

SOCRATES. And the act of carrying the cup, has – well, the innate quality of carrying something?

EUTHYPHRO. Yes, I suppose so –

SOCRATES. Good! We're getting somewhere.

EUTHYPHRO. Are we?

SOCRATES. What is carried is being carried. It is an absolute quality.

EUTHYPHRO. Yes.

SOCRATES. Of the cup.

EUTHYPHRO. Yes.

SOCRATES. And the act of carrying the cup, has the innate quality of carrying something.

EUTHYPHRO. Yes.

SOCRATES. Care to summarise?

EUTHYPHRO. Well, in the way it's the bleeding obvious – which, Socrates, if you'll forgive me, it often is with you. All you are saying is that there's a quality called 'carrying', and it can be in a thing that is carried and in the person who is carrying – the thing.

SOCRATES. Exactly! And you agree holiness is a quality?

EUTHYPHRO. Not quite with you there –

SOCRATES. Well, for example, a prayer is, in itself, holy?

EUTHYPHRO. Yes –

SOCRATES. And the act of making the prayer is, itself, a holy act?

EUTHYPHRO. Yes –

SOCRATES. Brilliant! So. We can say that a temple has the absolute quality of holiness.

EUTHYPHRO. Yes, a temple is holy –

SOCRATES. And going to a temple, is a holy act –

EUTHYPHRO. Yes –

SOCRATES. And the gods are holy.

EUTHYPHRO. Yes –

SOCRATES. Every god is holy.

EUTHYPHRO. Arguing with you, one always ends up saying 'yes, Socrates' –

SOCRATES. Nearly there. And every act of a god is holy?

EUTHYPHRO. Yes, Socrates!

SOCRATES. And here we are outside the magistrates' court, because we agree justice is holy?

EUTHYPHRO. We do.

SOCRATES. And that just acts are holy.

EUTHYPHRO. And criminal acts, unjust acts, are unholy.

SOCRATES. Yes! So, tell me, my dear religious friend, in the Trojan War, when the goddess Athena said justice was on the side of the Greeks, and the god Apollo said justice was on the side of the Trojans, which of them was right?

EUTHYPHRO *stares at him.*

Because if Athena, who is holy, was right to support the Greeks, then Apollo, who is also a holy god, was acting in an unholy way.

(*A beat.*) Or the reverse.

EUTHYPHRO *is in severe discomfort.*

One of the two gods was acting in an unholy way. Yes?

EUTHYPHRO. Well. Well. What really matters is – is that in the war, Zeus, father of the gods, was neutral.

SOCRATES. You mean Zeus was neither holy nor unholy?

EUTHYPHRO. No. Yes. No. It's – a mystery.

SOCRATES. But not acting is, in itself, an action. Are you saying that Zeus was being both holy and unholy at the same time?

EUTHYPHRO. Look, this is religion! It is a mystery!

SOCRATES. I would call it a contradiction.

EUTHYPHRO. It is beyond our comprehension, because the gods wish it to be so!

SOCRATES. Because they are holy.

EUTHYPHRO. Yes! Yes!

SOCRATES. So whatever they do, is holy?

EUTHYPHRO. Yes!

SOCRATES. Even if it is supporting an unjust war?

EUTHYPHRO (*flicker*). Yes!

SOCRATES. So there is no innate holiness in justice itself, it depends on which god supports which cause –

EUTHYPHRO. I –

SOCRATES. Or maybe since a god is holy, whatever he or she does must be holy, even if it's supporting an unjust war –

EUTHYPHRO. Er, no no –

SOCRATES. Or turning into a bull, snatching a young woman from a beach and taking her to Crete to rape her? As Zeus did to Europa?

EUTHYPHRO. This is dangerous!

SOCRATES. Why, because the rape of Europa was unjust? Zeus himself committed an unholy act?

EUTHYPHRO. Just stop stop stop! My!

He laughs, though he is sweating. An uneasy glance away to make sure no one is listening to them.

I mean, an argument with you, Socrates – it's, well, rather like being caught in a funnel-web spider's web, the further you go in, the tighter things get.

SOCRATES. Oh my dear fellow, I'm sorry you feel that. But with spiders' webs one can just –

A clearing away gesture.

So it should be with our enquiries, our musings about the world, us in it, from the profound to the trivial – what is light? Why does my bottom itch?

EUTHYPHRO. Indeed yes, it's all only words, isn't it. This philosophising. Quite harmless.

SOCRATES. Absolutely. How can truth do harm?

He beams.

And light is the presence of god. And the itch is a little flea.

EUTHYPHRO *recovering breath.*

EUTHYPHRO. Yes. Yes. Oh my. A good canter round the course there, Socrates! (*A breath.*) So, so – why are you outside the magistrates' court?

SOCRATES. Oh something trivial, though perhaps it'll be amusing. I've come to see about an indictment. They're setting a date for the trial.

EUTHYPHRO *does not take this seriously.*

EUTHYPHRO. I can't imagine you bringing a charge against anyone!

SOCRATES. Certainly not. Never accuse, just question. Much better way to get up people's noses!

EUTHYPHRO. So it's you to go on trial. But what's this about? Have you fallen in love with someone you shouldn't?

SOCRATES. Oh nothing so glamorous, nothing so dangerous. I am charged with denying the gods exist and inventing new ones.

EUTHYPHRO *is stunned.*

EUTHYPHRO. Sacrilege?

SOCRATES. That's the main meal.

EUTHYPHRO. There's another charge?

SOCRATES. They've thrown in a little pastry as dessert – I'm also accused of corrupting the young.

EUTHYPHRO. Well, who of us hasn't at some time – but *sacrilege*? My dear fellow, it's –

SOCRATES. A death-penalty offence, yes.

SOCRATES *grins.*

EUTHYPHRO. You seem amazingly – breezy – about it.

SOCRATES. To make a speech for your life to a jury of five hundred and one fellow citizens? Under the blue sky of our Athenian spring, standing beside a water clock, each word a drip of water? As I said, it could be amusing.

EUTHYPHRO. But this is an outrage! How can you be so flippant?

SOCRATES. Oh – be flippant about death. Only be serious about things we can change. Five hundred and one! No chance a verdict can be a dead heat! I love the rules of our democracy, their hard-edged clarity.

EUTHYPHRO. The laws may have clear edges, people don't. I fear bluntness is a human condition. But no jury, surely however fanatic, or bored, would – I mean the case against you, it must be a practical joke – someone got drunk, went to the magistrate – do you know who?

SOCRATES. His name's Meletus. I don't know him, but I've seen him about – young, long hair, not much of a beard, aquiline nose. A good-looking boy and cocky with it – but a pissed, practical joker? I think not. It's great that the young take right-thinking so seriously. Get rid of the likes of me, he says, keep the city safe from impious thinking. Maybe he's got a point!

EUTHYPHRO. I think not. Attacking you will do terrible damage to our freedoms. And 'corrupting the young'? How does he say you do that?

SOCRATES (*shrugs*). Well, clearly I upset him. And the young believe it's their absolute right not to be upset.

EUTHYPHRO. But to use religion against you –

SOCRATES. No no, this is a passionate young man, he says he's protecting the gods.

EUYTHPRO. As if they need protecting from a man with no shoes!

SOCRATES. Yes! Maybe this isn't about religion at all, it's about me not wearing shoes. (*Finger raised.*) Interesting. Norms. The normal. The loathing of deviation.

EUTHYPHRO. Though, I mean – I can see –

SOCRATES. Can see what?

EUTHYPHRO. I mean you can be –

SOCRATES. Can be what?

EUTHYTHRO. You do keep on about how you receive divine signs.

SOCRATES. Can't do anything about that. It's my inner daemon, speaking to me.

EUTHYPHRO. But banging on about it allows your enemies to say you claim to have a god within you, overriding all others.

SOCRATES. The daemon only tells me when I'm wrong. But I do bang on, I give you that. It's such fun.

EUTHYPHRO. Fun? Your 'banging on' is dangerous, can't you see where it leads? Deny the gods are holy and – you deny they are gods –

SOCRATES. So you think Meletus may have a point –

EUTHYPHRO. I mean just now – Zeus on Crete – you can't say things like that –

SOCRATES. But I did say that –

EUTHYPHRO. The ways of the gods are beyond our comprehension –

SOCRATES. I agree. The most important thing to know is that we know nothing. But –

EUTHYPHRO. Don't say 'but'! Don't! With you 'but' is a lethal word!

SOCRATES. You said words are harmless.

EUTHYPHRO. Not that one!

SOCRATES. Relax, my dear. We've come to the courts for justice. Which is simply about the good. I mean that goodness between us.

EUTHYPHRO. Yes, yes, let's say that –

SOCRATES. So all we have to do is ask what do we call 'good'? And is it holy?

EUTHYPHRO *recoils.*

EUTHYPHRO. No, oh, er, no look I have to be somewhere –

SOCRATES. But we can go into the magistrates' together, and carry on talking –

EUTHYPHRO. Oh gods gods – no, just remembered, there's something I must do first –

SOCRATES. Another time?

EUTHYPHRO. Yes.

SOCRATES. Please send my best wishes to your wife.

EUTHYPHRO. Yes.

SOCRATES *turns away.*

Socrates.

SOCRATES *turns back.*

SOCRATES. Yes?

EUTHYPHRO. I beg you. Be careful.

SOCRATES, *smiling.*

SOCRATES. Why?

End of Scene One.

Scene Two: Home Vs World

Antechamber of the law court in the Agora.

XANTHIPPE *sits very still. Before her there is a small table, on it there are pastries.*

A silence.

Enter ASPASIA. *She is carrying a flat basket covered by a cloth. She removes the cloth.*

They look at each other's bakes.

ASPASIA. Birds' nests.

XANTHIPPE. Honey pastries.

A pause.

ASPASIA. Has Meletus – ?

XANTHIPPE. I think he's spoken.

ASPASIA. Any idea how –

XANTHIPPE. There were some laughs.

ASPASIA (*concerned*). You mean he went down well?

XANTHIPPE. How can I know?

ASPASIA. Ah the courts, the gymnasia, the theatres, the private drinking parties, the all-male world.

XANTHIPPE. Which you love.

ASPASIA. Not love. Pity.

XANTHIPPE. Oh, come off it –

ASPASIA. No, the men, poor things! Youths sloshing on body oils to hide that crotch-sweat smell, and statesmen on their knees in the gymnasia, looking at the impression of a boy's balls in the sand.

XANTHIPPE. I'm surprised you don't put on a beard and join in.

ASPASIA. I've had my moments.

XANTHIPPE. I bet you have.

ASPASIA *laughs and turns away to the entrance, looking out to the court. Musing.*

ASPASIA. Do you think you could rig a jury?

XANTHIPPE. Bribe five hundred people?

ASPASIA. I mean rig the selection.

XANTHIPPE. But the kleroterion choses jurors at random.

ASPASIA. The kleroterion's a machine. Machines can be fixed.

XANTHIPPE. That's unthinkable!

ASPASIA. Unthinkable thoughts come in unthinkable times.

XANTHIPPE. You don't for a moment –

ASPASIA. No no, of course not.

ASPASIA *turns back to the pastries.*

How do you get the pastry to go like twigs?

XANTHIPPE. I roll the dough see-through thin, cut it very fine, then I fry it in deep oil, very fast, you have to concentrate or the strands will burn.

ASPASIA. Sounds like a religious rite.

XANTHIPPE. There's no mystery, just practice and elbow grease, you know, like life.

ASPASIA. Indeed.

After a pause XANTHIPPE *cannot resist asking.*

XANTHIPPE. So what's that?

ASPASIA. The recipe's from Egypt, it's called baklava.

XANTHIPPE. How do you get the flaky layers to curl?

ASPASIA. I've no idea. A slave made them.

XANTHIPPE. Probably by brushing on layers of clarified butter.

ASPASIA. You're making the point I have never cooked anything in my life, right?

Enter EUTHYPHRO *at pace.*

EUTHYPHRO. All good! All good!

ASPASIA. And Socrates –

EUTHYPHRO. Up on the platform now, charming them – relaxed, gracious, sticking to the rhetorical forms. The atmosphere's a little tense but – it's absolutely fine.

ASPASIA. And Meletus –

EUTHYPHRO. What you'd expect.

XANTHIPPE. I heard them laugh –

EUTHYPHRO. At him, not with him.

ASPASIA. He went down badly?

EUTHYPHRO. It was a rant. What is happening to the young? Hopeless oratory, Meletus managed to whine and shout at the same time.

ASPASIA. Whine and shout about –

EUTHYPHRO. Oh ridiculous stuff, self-centred, self-regarding – not worth repeating.

ASPASIA. Indulge us.

EUTHYPHRO. Where to begin –

He makes a dismissive wave of the hand.

The speech was an incoherent mess, but he seemed to be saying that – that the very way Socrates speaks is offensive. It doesn't matter what questions he asks, what they are about, just hearing them corrupts your mind, makes you doubt even the existence of the gods.

ASPASIA. Well –

EUTHYPHRO. Yes yes, he's made me wobble at times – I think it's his sense of fun –

XANTHIPPE, *leaden.*

XANTHIPPE. Fun.

EUTHYPHRO. But Meletus lost his audience. He was too extreme. Socrates targets the sons of famous men! Pimps them to enemies of the state at drinking parties! Sons of famous men are spouting doubts about everything, even the need to wear shoes! Socrates is a conspiracy! He is an atheist! A blasphemer! He consorts with witches!

XANTHIPPE, *looking at* ASPASIA.

XANTHIPPE. Whom can he mean?

EUTHYPHRO. Look there's absolutely nothing to worry about. Some grandee will have put Meletus up to this.

ASPASIA. I suspect that pompous fool, Anytus.

EUTHYPHRO. Yes! You could be right. Socrates and his son were – close.

XANTHIPPE (*low*). All the shoeless boys, in and out of the house.

EUTHYPHRO. Personal spite should never get mixed up with politics.

ASPASIA. But it always is.

XANTHIPPE. I don't find this reassuring –

EUTHYPHRO. No no. All your husband has to do is round off his speech by apologising – 'If I've caused offence, blah and blah', then everyone can have a good gossip and go home. I must get back, mustn't miss the climax!

And then just a flicker of anxiety.

We are fine. Yes!

He exits quickly.

XANTHIPPE. He's scared.

ASPASIA. It will be all right.

XANTHIPPE. Oh well, you know, don't you. You are in the swim. The great sea of politicking – seeing who can drown whom.

ASPASIA. I don't want to quarrel, Xanthippe.

XANTHIPPE. No? Oh, pity –

ASPASIA. I mean, not today –

XANTHIPPE. But it's a very good day to quarrel with my husband's whore of forty years' standing. Seeing it's your fault he's on trial for his life.

ASPASIA. You know that's not true.

XANTHIPPE. Do I? You know what I know, do you? Oh the great courtesan's knowingness, the leering look –

ASPASIA. Don't do the wronged woman, I mean you've been doing it since the first day you – but please not now, we've got to be in this together –

XANTHIPPE. And what 'this' is that?

ASPASIA. Oh sex, fidelity, who's having who, when the world's falling apart, what does it matter?

XANTHIPPE. 'Falling apart'?

ASPASIA. Socrates on trial? A few years ago that would have been unthinkable.

XANTHIPPE. So you admit he's in danger –

ASPASIA. Of course it's dangerous –

XANTHIPPE. Oh big woman in the know, you said it'll all be fine!

ASPASIA. It's a game! A game we can win, as long as we're all as one.

XANTHIPPE. Oh, yes, you'd love that, wouldn't you. 'All as one', the fantasy of the adulterer and the mistress – a threesome with the wife. Love as a neat little – (*Gesture, palms of her hand.*) pitty-patty meatball of rolled-up flesh.

(*Raises hands in prayer looking up.*) Do you hear me, Aphrodite of the Pines, today of all days, get this bitch out of my life!

ASPASIA. Xanthippe, if only you –

XANTHIPPE. What, wanted to go to bed with you? Like my husband?

ASPASIA. If only you –

She stops.

XANTHIPPE. If only I what?

ASPASIA. No –

XANTHIPPE. Oh come on –

ASPASIA. If only you could see what we are, you and I!

XANTHIPPE. And what are we?

ASPASIA. Rare, Xanthippe. Very rare. We won't be merely remembered as daughter of him or him or him, wife of him or him – the people of the future will know our names! Hundreds of years from now, our shadows will still be on earth.

XANTHIPPE. 'Our shadows will still – '

She blows a raspberry.

Oh famous names, people, battles, trials, Athens and the Empire, Marathon, war with Sparta, all that noise, yes that'll be remembered. But what really matters is always forgotten – who cooked, who cleaned, who stopped a child swallowing a stone.

ASPASIA. But there are slaves to cook, clean, nanny the stone-swallowers. We're high-born, privileged women! We have a duty beyond domesticity.

XANTHIPPE. Our greatest duty is to the family.

ASPASIA. Our greatest duty is to the state.

XANTHIPPE. The 'state', horrid word! When I hear it I see a great wall of mud and men, about to come crashing down on me.

ASPASIA. And when I hear 'family' I see –

Stops.

XANTHIPPE. What?

ASPASIA. A noose, I see a noose, tightening round a woman's neck. In an execution chamber called 'the family home'. Can't you see the gods have commanded you and me –

XANTHIPPE. Oh yuck –

ASPASIA. Yes, commanded us to use our lives, beyond cook-pots and potty training.

XANTHIPPE. Yuck yuck yuck, 'command', a big horrid state word, rolling over everything, grinding us to bits.

ASPASIA. We've no choice, ground to bits or not. The gods have made us the guardians of a great soul.

XANTHIPPE. 'Great soul'? My husband is a – ? I mean I expect a woman like you to boast about guarding his dick, but his *soul*?

ASPASIA. Blame the daughters of Ananke, but that's what we are.

XANTHIPPE. Oh yes, the way out, 'Before the Fates I am nothing.' Well, I *am* something, I'm me! Your 'public life', your 'state', it's not real –

ASPASIA. Oh it's real enough! What do you think's happening out there? The state is trying to tear down a – yes, yes, a great soul –

XANTHIPPE. But what can I do? I just put my trust in my household gods. I'll stay by my hearth, my children in my arms. All that is real to me is a kiss, a smile on their little faces. Against all that cruelty, the state, your politics, you can't live in it, that's why it's not real, a political idea isn't a house!

ASPASIA. I know how you feel, but –

XANTHIPPE. You can't know how I feel. You've never had children.

ASPASIA. The price I've paid.

XANTHIPPE. Yes yes, the price of stuffing palm oil and pomegranate up yourself –

ASPASIA. I've served my country –

XANTHIPPE. You mean serviced powerful men!

ASPASIA. It's grand of me to say this, but why not, why should we not be grand? Why shouldn't a woman have a place in the councils of life and death?

XANTHIPPE. Life and – (*Scoffs.*) Only mothers know how fierce, how absolute they are, life and death. They watch each other across a newborn baby's bed. Life in one corner, afraid of death, who slinks around the walls, jealous of anything that lives. And there's always that sick feeling even in your dreams, is he all right? You wake, is he breathing, still warm? And you'd give everything, you'd give your blood, to keep them safe.

ASPASIA. Bit of a poetess, aren't we, these second-rate images – for fucksake, woman! Don't you have any idea what is at stake here?

XANTHIPPE. Of course I do! Because of this trial my sons will be branded the children of a criminal father, executed for sacrilege!

ASPASIA. That's not going to happen.

XANTHIPPE. Yes it is. I can hear the spirits, whispering it, giggling –

ASPASIA. Oh! No no, your spirits must be the vicious kind.

XANTHIPPE. Kind or vicious, they're never wrong.

ASPASIA. Xanthippe, I didn't realise that you – look, there's not the faintest possibility they'll actually sentence him.

XANTHIPPE. But his accuser, this Meletus, he's a fanatic.

ASPASIA. Fanatics are like iron. In the end they rust and crumble.

XANTHIPPE. I don't think so. The assembly's full of farmers, their fields burnt by Sparta. Pig-ignorant, out of their minds, looking for a sacrifice, someone to blame for the gods of their fields deserting them! And there is my husband. Sitting there. Being clever. Saying annoying things.

ASPASIA. Your spirits have some political acumen. But no no! Meletus and his mad dogs will be voted down, exposed, shown to be the lunatics they are. Laughed at, ridiculed.

XANTHIPPE. So it's not about life and death at all.

ASPASIA. The trial's a tactic.

XANTHIPPE. Tactic.

ASPASIA. But we've got to keep our nerve, get it right. It's a political game.

XANTHIPPE. Really? What, dice, rolled on the city streets? My family, rolled in the gutter in a 'game' of chance?

ASPASIA *loses her temper.*

ASPASIA. Oh family family family! Warm little limbs in cradle, Mummy and Daddy guardians by the hearthside – the family huddled together safe behind, what? The city wall. But who builds the wall, maintains it, mounts the guards? The state.

XANTHIPPE. And I'm a state heroine, yes? An oven on legs for making soldiers, serving up sons for death to dine on? In his taverns along your wall!

ASPASIA. Death's taverns – dear oh dear, you are writing poems. Can't you see the state protects you?

XANTHIPPE. No, the state oppresses me.

ASPASIA. No, the state's the common good, the democratic will of all of us!

XANTHIPPE. No, it's the will of men in secret rooms. Helped by a whore who writes their speeches. How can you be content just to be – an ingredient in their half-baked ideas?

ASPASIA. My dear, in the past I've been the whole cake!

XANTHIPPE. Yes, they say Pericles caught democracy from you in bed.

ASPASIA. I know. (*She smiles.*) The most powerful ideas can come from caresses in the dark. In many ways I did invent democratic Athens. Had to fuck the brains out of Pericles to do it. But that was no hardship, he was a beautiful man.

XANTHIPPE. And a ruthless bastard.

ASPASIA. Absolutely.

XANTHIPPE. And was my husband's speech whispered to him with caresses?

ASPASIA. Oh, that's all gone. It's your turn for the pillow stuff.

XANTHIPPE. Oh thank you, kind lady!

ASPASIA. All things pass. 'And I have lived and loved, and closed the door.'

XANTHIPPE. Sappho.

ASPASIA. Yes. (*A beat.*) Why must we quarrel?

XANTHIPPE. Isn't that obvious?

ASPASIA. I mean, over a man, granted your husband but –

XANTHIPPE. We're not quarrelling over a man, we're quarrelling over how to live.

ASPASIA. Yes. (*She sighs.*) Yes, we are.

A pause.

XANTHIPPE. So you wrote what he's saying out there?

ASPASIA. I drafted something – politic.

XANTHIPPE. Politic. And it'll 'play the game', get him off, yes?

ASPASIA. He just has to read it, with his usual flair, of course.

XANTHIPPE. Do you mean read –

She lifts a scroll that has been concealed beside her.

This?

ASPASIA. Oh. No. Oh! What's he saying out there?

XANTHIPPE. He's improvising, of course.

ASPASIA. I told him, just for once, this time, stick to the text!

XANTHIPPE. Has he ever? You think he has some grand scheme, with his philosophy? He doesn't. He just – thinks as he speaks.

ASPASIA. Listen!

A pause.

XANTHIPPE. Are they cheering, are they booing, are they –

ASPASIA. I can't tell.

Enter SOCRATES. *He is smiling and in excellent spirits. He makes straight for the pastries.*

SOCRATES. Ah, birds' nests. And what are these?

XANTHIPPE. Some Egyptian crap.

Picks one up and is eating.

SOCRATES. Mm! Pistachio.

They are glaring at him.

ASPASIA. Well?

Enter EUTHYPHRO*, angry.*

EUTHYPHRO. Socrates, in the name of the living gods, what do you think you're doing? –

ASPASIA. How bad – ?

EUTHYPHRO. Why did you have to bring up the Delphic Oracle?

XANTHIPPE. Oh no.

ASPASIA. Of all things – why get on to that?

SOCRATES, *still eating.*

SOCRATES. Well the Oracle was asked, 'Who is the wisest man living?' And she did reply 'Socrates.' So I argued I shouldn't be put to death because I am so very wise.

He licks his fingers.

EUTHYPHRO. Is it a death wish with you? Do you want Hades?

SOCRATES. There would be interesting conversations.

ASPASIA (*to* EUTHYPHRO). How damaging do you think –

EUTHYPHRO. I don't know, the public mood can swing so quickly –

SOCRATES. Yes, in Hades I could ask Homer if he believes we are god-driven, or whether we have free will.

EUTHYPHRO (*to* SOCRATES). It was your tone, the light-hearted contempt –

SOCRATES (*licking his fingers*). 'Free will' in any meaningful sense.

EUTHYPHRO. I mean, do you want a guilty verdict? Just for an effect?

SOCRATES *helps himself to another pastry.*

SOCRATES. No no, I love the good things of life too much. But if that be a pursuit that has put me at risk, so be it.

XANTHIPPE. Can we! Please! Please! Just for moment!

They are still.

A pause.

(*Trying to be calm.*) Don't you see, it's not just you at risk, not just you.

SOCRATES. My dear – remember the eagle with a tortoise in its claws. It flew over a theatre. At that moment the playwright Aeschylus was rehearsing one of his immortal works. The eagle –

XANTHIPPE. – dropped the tortoise which hit him on the head and killed him on the spot yes yes –

EUTHYPHRO. Where are we going with this?

ASPASIA. Risk is random. Even ridiculous.

XANTHIPPE. Oh yes oh yes, oh yes! Hold on to reason, even though your fingernails are breaking –

SOCRATES. Exactly! That's why I spoke of the Oracle. When she was asked, 'Who is the wisest man alive?' what did she reply? 'Socrates.' Does Socrates say he is wise? No. In what way does he say he is not wise? He says he knows nothing. But if the wisest man living knows nothing, what does everyone else know? Nothing. That is the wisdom that we all have to learn. That we know nothing. (*A beat.*) Totally rational, you see.

He bites into a pastry.

EUTHYPHRO *waves his hands.*

EUTHYPHRO. Well, we must hope Apollo god of reason is whispering to the jury. I must see how the vote – yes.

He exits.

XANTHIPPE. You couldn't say no.

SOCRATES. I have to do what she says.

ASPASIA. But you didn't do what I said! That's the problem! I told you, once in your life, be politic! Make a simple apology! You didn't do what I said!

XANTHIPPE (*scoffs*). Listen to that! (*To* ASPASIA.) It may come as a shock but – actually we're not talking about you.

ASPASIA. He's listening to someone else?

XANTHIPPE. Oh yes.

ASPASIA (*to* SOCRATES). You've not been talking to Diotima – I warned you about that cow.

XANTHIPPE (*to* SOCRATES). Who is Diotima?

SOCRATES. An acquaintance –

ASPASIA. A dancer who thinks she can think.

SOCRATES. She's interesting for how she lives –

XANTHIPPE (*to* ASPASIA). Oh you mean one of his little Sapphic girlfriends? No we're not talking about her. (*To* SOCRATES.) Just once, just for today, tell it to go away –

SOCRATES. I can't. Sometimes it is you.

XANTHIPPE. No no no no, don't do that, don't lay that on me –

SOCRATES. You hear it too.

XANTHIPPE. But to me it says the opposite.

SOCRATES. No we just hear differently.

ASPASIA. What – oh. Is this that thing?

SOCRATES *and* XANTHIPPE *are suddenly looking at her as one – the first time in the scene.*

A pause.

The daemon thing?

They are still.

Oh come on, it's not real – 'Oh I have a god, goddess, voice inside me so I can do no other?' Making out you're in touch with the divine, don't you see how that riles people? When it's just a cheap trick to clinch arguments.

XANTHIPPE. You don't –

SOCRATES. A trick? Mm. If it is I'm not playing it, it's being played on me –

EUTHYPHRO *enters at speed.*

EUTHYPHRO. A majority of sixty-one.

A silence.

ASPASIA. Sixty-one.

XANTHIPPE. So it's over?

ASPASIA. Narrow.

XANTHIPPE. Over.

ASPASIA. But an acquittal's an acquittal.

XANTHIPPE. Aphrodite, Aphrodite, I am in your debt –

EUTHYPHRO. Not acquittal! They found him guilty.

A silence.

XANTHIPPE. No.

ASPASIA. That can't be.

XANTHIPPE. No.

EUTHYPHRO. It's the verdict.

ASPASIA. This is a civilised country!

EUTHYPHRO. No longer. We're turning on the best amongst us.

XANTHIPPE. No. No. No. No.

SOCRATES. My dear.

XANTHIPPE. Don't 'my dear' me! The more terrible the news, the more you 'my dear' me!

EUTHYPHRO. Please, all is not lost –

ASPASIA. No, we'll win the vote on mitigating the sentence –

EUTHYPHRO. Absolutely.

XANTHIPPE. The stupidity, stupidity of you all, stupidity, stupidity.

She sits, staring ahead.

ASPASIA *makes a move to comfort her but* SOCRATES *shakes his head. She stops.*

SOCRATES *turns away.*

ASPASIA. Right.

EUTHYPHRO. Yes, what to –

ASPASIA. Sixty-one votes.

EUTHYPHRO. Yes.

ASPASIA. Thirty-one jurors. You must twist arms, offer a loan here and there, a girl, a boy –

EUTHYPHRO. I thought appeal to their honour.

ASPASIA. Try that too.

EUTHYPHRO. I'll do my best, but time – it all depends on –

ASPASIA. The second speech, yes.

They look anxiously at SOCRATES. *He is oblivious of them, sunk in his thoughts.*

EUTHYPHRO. He'll have to offer to pay a fine.

ASPASIA. Yes.

EUTHYPHRO. It has to be big. If he is to avoid exile as well.

ASPASIA. To the order of – what?

EUTHYPHRO. Thirty minas?

ASPASIA. That's what I'm thinking.

EUTHYPHRO. Socrates –

XANTHIPPE. Stupidity! Of all the talk, the drinking, the young men around you in the open air at your feet, laughing, their elders watching from a distance, hating, plotting – and now this! How can we possibly get –

ASPASIA. Oh I have favours of a lifetime to pull in. Which I will do. For him. For you. For your children. For what we believe in.

SOCRATES *is suddenly fully engaged again.*

SOCRATES. It's elegant of them, isn't it.

They are lost.

EUTHYPHRO. Elegant of –

SOCRATES. The laws. To allow a convicted prisoner to suggest his own sentence.

EUTHYPHRO. Yes yes, and this is an open door. Just thirty-one votes out of the five hundred and one. I'm sure no one but the core of fanatics – maybe just Meletus, his relatives – tribe members – I mean hardly anyone wants the death sentence actually carried out. They just want to clip your wings and, knowing you, you'll grow new ones in a day! So, what's in order is – you praise the court to the skies, extoll its wisdom, the laws of the city, their divinity, their justice. And offer to pay the fine. Announce the amount with a suitable – flourish. Weeping would be good but I don't think we can quite expect that of you!

SOCRATES (*smiles*). No I don't think that would convince. (*To* ASPASIA.) What do we believe? That's why I ask questions. (*To* XANTHIPPE.) And yes. I am stupid. Because I haven't found the answers.

XANTHIPPE. Oh so pat, so – just – leave all that! Stop. Stop. The thinking. For once.

SOCRATES. Yes.

ASPASIA. Be contrite.

SOCRATES. Yes, contrite.

ASPASIA. Apologise.

SOCRATES. I will.

A pause.

SOCRATES *smiles. They are uneasy.*

EUTHYPHRO. The court will be back in session, we must go.

XANTHIPPE. I know what you're doing.

SOCRATES *and* XANTHIPPE*, locked in eye contact.*

Just stop it, just for a while, the next few minutes. For our family. For me. For yourself, you silly, silly, sweet fool of a man. Do the simple thing.

SOCRATES. The simple thing, so hard to achieve. Yes. (*A beat.*) Then tonight we will all go out in the Agora for dinner!

He beams and exits with EUTHYPHRO.

A silence.

ASPASIA. What is he doing?

XANTHIPPE *does not reply.*

You said you know.

XANTHIPPE*, again, nothing.*

You and him, I've never understood.

XANTHIPPE. Go with the wagging tongues. Fame-hungry virgin hooks famous old lecher.

ASPASIA. I've never believed the tongues.

XANTHIPPE. No?

ASPASIA. You're much more than that.

XANTHIPPE. Well, thank you very much.

A pause. Very wary of each other.

ASPASIA. If you understand what he's doing, tell me. Maybe it'll help, even now.

XANTHIPPE. I did tell you. He improvises.

ASPASIA. That's not – none of us just make ourselves up on the spot.

XANTHIPPE. Men do, haven't you noticed? Or think they do.

ASPASIA. Your family had you down as a priestess, didn't they, you were going to be with the temple of Aphrodite.

XANTHIPPE (*scoffs*). What, and he rescued me? No.

ASPASIA. You think you rescued him?

XANTHIPPE. Oh I'm afraid we're beyond saving ourselves. Really afraid.

A pause.

XANTHIPPE *is very tired.* ASPASIA *is increasingly annoyed.*

ASPASIA. It's bloody religion, isn't it. I've always felt that with him, there's a – mist inside him. For all his rationality. A – squidginess. And he is on trial for denying the gods!

XANTHIPPE (*weary*). Yes, yes.

ASPASIA. I mean this daemon, what does it actually say?

XANTHIPPE *shrugs.*

XANTHIPPE. Most of the time it says 'no'.

ASPASIA. Let's hope it's saying 'no' to playing the fool out there right now.

XANTHIPPE. You don't see them, do you.

ASPASIA. 'Them'?

XANTHIPPE. The spirits.

ASPASIA. Oh for fucksake.

XANTHIPPE. Look!

She holds up a hand.

The ends of your fingers! Can't you see them, dancing?

ASPASIA. Superstition.

XANTHIPPE. I believe in 'superstition'.

ASPASIA. We're trying to get rid of all that crap!

XANTHIPPE. Oh the rational 'know thyself' Athens. That's all gone.

ASPASIA. No it's what we're trying to hang on to –

XANTHIPPE, *reviving, feeding off* ASPASIA*'s annoyance.*

XANTHIPPE. It's too late. The dream you and Pericles had, it failed. 'The great Athenian world order', oh how I hate those slogans. It's Meletus's time now. Witch-hunting, pulling down the old truths, he and his kind, they've got blood in their nostrils. In a way I feel – why not?

ASPASIA. You don't believe in the struggle to preserve democracy?

XANTHIPPE. I've told you what I 'struggle to preserve'.

ASPASIA. Oh family and home-cooking and fireside gods and spirits.

XANTHIPPE. There's nothing more important than family.

ASPASIA. We have made history in Athens!

XANTHIPPE. There's no such thing as history, only people's lives.

ASPASIA. Ha! Who said that? Some oracle, some priestess, off her head?

XANTHIPPE. All women were priestesses once.

ASPASIA. I don't want to be a priestess, I want to be –

She stops dead.

XANTHIPPE. What? A ruler? A queen? A tyrant?

ASPASIA. A citizen.

XANTHIPPE *holds up her hand, palm out to* ASPASIA.

XANTHIPPE. Look. They're laughing.

Enter SOCRATES.

He is relaxed, smiling.

ASPASIA. Well?

SOCRATES, *forefinger up in the typical gesture.*

SOCRATES. Simplicity achieved.

Enter EUTHYPHRO, *distressed.*

EUTHYPHRO. Forgive me.

SOCRATES. For what, dear man?

EUTHYPHRO. You make it impossible.

SOCRATES. On the contrary, I'm opening possibilities –

EUTHYPHRO. That's rubbish! No one will listen to you now – after – after that –

He is breathless, hand to his chest.

ASPASIA. After what?

EUTHYPHRO. I can no longer – I've done all I can to protect you, though I find you the most difficult, repulsive man I ever – but I did it for our tribe, for the good of the city, for the old values of decency of – but no longer. No.

XANTHIPPE (*to* SOCRATES).What have you done?

SOCRATES. I suggested my just punishment.

XANTHIPPE. The fine?

EUTHYPHRO. You're mocking us. That's all your teaching comes down to, mockery. Well – mocked I have been. I must look to myself now. My family. What's left of my reputation.

ASPASIA. You're deserting us? At the very moment they are voting for the sentence? Then go, with all the other rats –

SOCRATES. No no no. Euthyphro, my friend. It's understandable that we act in our own self-interest. The real question is – is acting in my self-interest, also acting to the dictate of what I know to be right?

EUTHYPHRO. Even at this moment – spinning a net in which we'll all strangle –

SOCRATES. It's not I who spin it, the net of God traps us all. Go – when the sentence is announced, Crito, Plato and the rest will be rushing in to shout at me. You did all you could.

EUTHYPHRO. Do you forgive me?

A moment's hiatus. He turns to go.

SOCRATES. You can only do that yourself. A life unexamined is not worth living.

EUTHYPHRO. Gods, gods – (*Turns on him.*) I don't want to examine myself! I'm me and I'm content with that, I'm me!

SOCRATES. Are you?

Exit EUTHYPHRO.

XANTHIPPE. What did you say to the court? Why should they – what was the sentence you asked for?

SOCRATES. It was a reasonable request.

ASPASIA. A smaller fine? Not exile –

SOCRATES. No. I asked to be condemned to having free dinners provided for me, by the state, for life.

A silence.

XANTHIPPE. Free – dinners?

ASPASIA *exits fast.*

A silence. XANTHIPPE *and* SOCRATES *are very still.*

They won't poison you.

SOCRATES. No?

XANTHIPPE. I'll sacrifice to Athena.

SOCRATES. Well, good.

XANTHIPPE. And I'll go to my sisters at Aphrodite's temple. We'll pray to her to intervene.

SOCRATES. Mm. It's said those two great goddesses are not the best of womanly friends –

XANTHIPPE (*shouts*). Shut up! Shut up! Silly! Silly! Stupid! Stupid! Stupid man! Playing your games, moving pebbles around in holes, words, words, just words!

A pause.

SOCRATES. I want you to leave Athens. I've sent messages, to the Pythagoreans, Plato's friends, in Syracuse. Religiously mad but you can trust your life, our sons' lives to them.

XANTHIPPE. No.

SOCRATES. I want you to.

XANTHIPPE. No.

SOCRATES. I command you to.

XANTHIPPE. Ha!

SOCRATES. I know at times we've not been – but I fear for you.

XANTHIPPE. Athena knows what you're doing.

SOCRATES. Which is?

XANTHIPPE. What you always do, what you can't stop yourself doing – testing everything to destruction. But she won't let you, because the gods are just.

SOCRATES. Are they?

ASPASIA, *entering*.

ASPASIA. We will manage this. We will. We will find a way.

XANTHIPPE. What's happened –

ASPASIA *won't look at her.*

Poison.

SOCRATES (*smiling*). Oh bright-eyed Athena.

ASPASIA. Regroup, find a way –

SOCRATES. Out of interest, what is the vote to poison me?

ASPASIA. A way out, there will be –

XANTHIPPE. What is the fucking vote?

A pause.

ASPASIA. One hundred and forty against three hundred and sixty-one. He's alienated another eighty-one voters.

SOCRATES. No free dinners then.

XANTHIPPE *sweeps the plates of pastries to the floor.*

SOCRATES *turns to the door as if people are coming in and gives a broad smile, arms held wide.*

Plato, my sweet boy, let me explain.

End of Scene Two.

Scene Three: Observing the Ritual

One month later. Cell.

A plate of pastries on a small table.

SOCRATES *in fetters. A* GAOLER *– thirty-five to forty, weathered, experienced – kneels before him, removing them.*

GAOLER (*aside*). Course we've had all the famous ones in here, I mean my old man did the great Pericles himself. He brought me in to see the famous 'father of the state', fallen so low, as they say. I was what, five, but I remember it very well – Pericles shouted 'Get that fucking kid out of here!' The mighty always panic in the end. But this one? For now it's like – well, it's like he likes it. Obviously he's here cos he's a disgusting old perve, but when he talks to you – I dunno, he's some kind of necromancer, he charms you. You're flattered but at the same time you feel – you're not really here. You're just something in his head.

Done, the GAOLER *steps back.* SOCRATES *massages his legs.*

In the following exchange, the GAOLER *hides the intelligence he has shown in his aside.*

SOCRATES. Oh so good, so good. The greater the pain, the greater the pleasure, don't you think?

GAOLER (*aside*). Here we go. (*To* SOCRATES.) Not really.

SOCRATES. But you know when something is cold, like water from a spring?

GAOLER. I do know cold water –

SOCRATES. So don't we know what is hot, because we know what is cold?

GAOLER (*shrugs*). Yeah.

SOCRATES. And, in that way, don't we judge all sensations against their opposites?

GAOLER. How do you mean?

SOCRATES. Think – of a pillow, you say this pillow's too hard, because you know what it would feel like if it were soft?

GAOLER. Spose.

SOCRATES. You know of hardness in a thing, because you know softness?

A beat.

GAOLER. Spose.

SOCRATES. And isn't that the same with emotions? Joy, sorrow; excitement, boredom; even love and hate?

GAOLER. Well. (*A beat.*) All you're saying is things are one thing or the other, maybe with a bit of in-between.

SOCRATES. Exactly! So, with pain and pleasure, aren't they the same, one sensation with two extremes? Pain can be in pleasure, pleasure can be in pain?

GAOLER. Look – I've tortured men, so to me this is all a bit airy-fairy.

SOCRATES. Oh the world is airy-fairy.

GAOLER. Beg to differ there. Looks pretty hard-edged to me.

SOCRATES. You're a fortunate man, to see clearly. For myself, things can seem obvious at first, then they go blurry.

A pause.

The GAOLER *is eyeing the plate of pastries.*

They're Egyptian. My friend brings them every day. She turns her fears for me into food. Please, eat!

GAOLER. They look odd.

SOCRATES. Or blurry?

SOCRATES *smiles.*

The GAOLER *hesitates for a moment, then takes a pastry.*

SOCRATES *watches him eat.*

Good?

GAOLER. Pistachio nuts. Good for the heart, they say.

SOCRATES. Probably not. Food is food. I know why you've removed the fetters.

GAOLER. I can't comment on that.

SOCRATES. The ship's returned.

GAOLER. Can't comment.

SOCRATES. The voyage to the Holy Island and back. It's a beautiful ritual, don't you think? But what does it mean?

And the GAOLER *has cracked,* SOCRATES *has sucked him in.*

GAOLER. Why does it have to mean anything? It's religion!

SOCRATES. But why does it happen?

GAOLER. The gods want it.

SOCRATES. So Apollo wants fourteen young men to set sail to his temple on Delos every year, sleep there, pray, offer libations, come back a month later. And here in Athens there is a great palaver, sacrifices in the city, processions, a lot of money spent. Forgive me, it's my nature, I know it's annoying, but I have to ask again – why?

GAOLER. Why's there *got* to be a why? It's the story. The King of Crete puts a curse on Athens – send seven young men and women every year to be eaten by the Minotaur or else.

SOCRATES. Enter Theseus –

The GAOLER, *relishing this, not sending it up, hands held out like an actor.*

GAOLER. Theseus, great hero of our city, kills the Minotaur but fucks the King of Crete's daughter and carries her off. To the anger of Apollo.

SOCRATES. Thus wreaking divine vengeance!

GAOLER. Yeah, great stuff.

SOCRATES. So, for centuries, come the spring, the ship sails to Delos to placate the god.

GAOLER. Luckily for you.

SOCRATES. Lucky for a while! (*Parodying actor gesture.*) No executions while the ship's away, keep the city pure!

GAOLER. Well, that's the ritual.

SOCRATES. It is indeed. (*He smiles.*) Tell me, as my executioner, what do you make of this interruption in your line of work?

GAOLER. Like I said, it's religion.

SOCRATES. So if the ship didn't sail to Delos every spring, would the god be angry with us?

GAOLER. Course.

SOCRATES. Angry in what way?

GAOLER. Plague? Earthquake? Driving you mad so you kill your son cos you think he's a deer, or something?

SOCRATES. Yes. A speciality of Dionysus.

GAOLER. Don't let's mess with that one.

SOCRATES. Indeed not.

GAOLER. It's great how the gods don't do things by halves.

SOCRATES. 'Honour to you, Lord Dionysus, the twice born.'

GAOLER. 'Honour to you, Lord.'

They make a religious gesture, holding hands up, palms forward – the equivalent of Christians crossing themselves.

They drop their hands.

A pause.

SOCRATES. So, when we neglect the rituals of the gods, they punish us?

GAOLER. You don't let up, do you –

SOCRATES. I can't, for me it's being awake. So, offend them, and the gods punish us?

GAOLER. Course! Look at you.

SOCRATES. You think I am being punished by the gods?

GAOLER. Obviously.

A pause.

SOCRATES. The ship, has it been sighted?

The GAOLER *hesitates.*

Come come. Has it been sighted or has it already docked?

The GAOLER *looks at the pastries.* SOCRATES *gestures 'help yourself'. The* GAOLER *takes one.*

GAOLER. It put in just after sunrise.

SOCRATES. Today is the day.

GAOLER. Yeah.

A pause.

SOCRATES. So. Why are the gods punishing me?

GAOLER. Not for me to –

SOCRATES. To say? Oh do! I won't take offence, after all I'm as good as dead.

SOCRATES, *expectant.*

GAOLER. Well – you're a blasphemer.

SOCRATES. In what way do I blaspheme?

GAOLER. Nah, c'mon.

SOCRATES. Tell me, how do I blaspheme?

GAOLER. I don't want to get into an argument – they tell you, y'know, never get personal with the meat.

A pause.

The GAOLER *– who actually is naturally garrulous – struggles with himself.*

SOCRATES *waits patiently, a slight smile.*

They say you're an atheist.

SOCRATES. And who is this 'they'?

GAOLER. Well, lots.

SOCRATES. Lots, where?

GAOLER. On the streets. You're notorious. Everyone knows you're a fucking god-denier.

SOCRATES. Do they? Everyone. Mm. What is commonly assumed is usually untrue –

GAOLER. The jury agreed you are, so that's that.

SOCRATES. Ah the jury. The majority! But what if the verdict was wrong?

GAOLER. Nah come on, every banged-up toff or derelict swears they're innocent.

SOCRATES. But you're seen me in this cell, praying to the gods. Just now, we honoured Dionysus. And, when I was free, every day I offered libations in the Agora. Are these the actions of a denier?

GAOLER. Well, you've got to be an hypocrite, haven't you.

SOCRATES. You mean I fake my prayers?

GAOLER. Yeah!

SOCRATES. You see two worshippers light herbs on an altar, stand with their hands raised, the smoke from both altars goes up to the realm of the gods – how can you tell if one is faking it, the other is not?

GAOLER. That's obvious.

SOCRATES. How?

GAOLER. The faker will have bad fortune.

SOCRATES. Like being condemned to death?

GAOLER. Yeah.

SOCRATES. Because of the jury's verdict?

GAOLER. Yeah.

SOCRATES. Which must be just?

GAOLER. Course.

SOCRATES. But what if the majority is wrong because, actually, they ignore the gods, they aren't religious at all? What if they're corrupt, full of hatred, self-interest, acting for private gain, or because they're bribed, or part of a political plot? Or what if they simply can't stand the prisoner on trial because of – his hairstyle? The great democratic, virtuous mass of the jury – what if *they* are faking it?

GAOLER. Well, they can't be wrong, can they?

SOCRATES. Why not?

GAOLER. Cos they're inspired by the gods!

SOCRATES. So the majority is always right?

GAOLER. Yeah! If it's not, the whole of fucking democracy collapses, don't it?!

SOCRATES. Well, there's a thing.

SOCRATES *is not smiling*.

A pause.

GAOLER. Right, now you tell me, you tell me. Why do you think you're brighter than the rest of us?

SOCRATES. Do I think that?

GAOLER. There, you're doing it now!

SOCRATES. Doing what?

GAOLER. Showing how bright you think you are!

SOCRATES. How am I doing that?

GAOLER. By that know-all thing! Asking questions in that know-all way that says you don't know the answer!

SOCRATES. But I don't know.

GAOLER. Nah come off it.

SOCRATES. I do assure you every morning I wake up, look out of the window and make no sense of the world at all. I told you, things are blurry to me, beyond blurry sometimes, I wake up to chaos. And blink. And look again. Every day I feel I have to begin all over again, to make sense of anything.

GAOLER. Bullshit. I know what you're doing.

SOCRATES. Oh! What am I doing?

GAOLER. Getting your fucking end away like the rest of us!

SOCRATES. You think we all act in our self-interest?

GAOLER. The fuck we do, yeah.

SOCRATES. And how do I do that?

GAOLER. No no I've had it. I'm not argy-bargying with you no more. People are sick of la-di-da know-it-all, privileged piss-heads, sounding off. There's a whole rats' nest of you in this city! And you, Socrates, you're the worst – trying to trap us in our heads, turn everything inside out. I mean that crap about you having a daemon in you.

SOCRATES. I do have a daemon in me. Don't you?

GAOLER. Course I don't, I'm normal!

SOCRATES. Normal. Is anyone?

GAOLER. I mean, in the end, what are you?

SOCRATES. In the end I'd love to know –

GAOLER. Then I'll tell you!

A pause.

The GAOLER, *the rage inside him stuck.*

SOCRATES. Ah my friend, there. That's the problem. Can you know others, when you don't know yourself?

The rage bursts.

GAOLER. Don't know myself? Crap! Course I know myself! You think you're special, the great mind, so different from us, so superior, with no shoes on, wearing stinking old clothes, stuck up in your basket pissing nonsense down on us.

SOCRATES, *delight.*

SOCRATES. Oh me in the basket, you've seen the play! When Aristophanes had me hanging up in the air, using jumping fleas to measure the sun! What point did you think he was making?

GAOLER. P-point? He was saying you're just one more clever-clever shit, lounging about at dinner parties, spouting rubbish, thinking you're fixing the world while you listen to slaves playing flutes and fiddle with boys.

SOCRATES. Ah sweet music, smooth bodies and sea-dark wine, the narrow paths to enlightenment –

GAOLER. Lightenment? Light? Enlight? Truth is you arty-farty thinkers, you look down your noses at the farmers on the jury, people like me, doing the dirty things, scraping a living, getting through the disaster years with nothing. I mean, don't you know what it's like – Socrates, you pass yourself off as some kind of man of the streets – but walk past your house! Oh yeah, modest door, straight on the pavement, all very democratic, very polis, but behind that civic crap you got your atrium, your slave kitchen in your basement, airy rooms above, draperies and statues, tarts painted up as sybils on the walls, all bare thighs and dripping fruit. And in my mind's eye I see you in there, cock of the hoop, at your dinner parties, luring in our youth, poisoning 'em with ideas and orgies, thinking the city's all yours by rights. Well, maybe it was before the plague, the war, but I've got news – it's our time now. We the great unenlightened, the great unwashed, we are Athens now. You and your kind, you're the enemies of democracy.

SOCRATES *has remained calm throughout this diatribe but the last remark makes him jump.*

SOCRATES. Oh. Now that is bad. How am I an enemy of democracy?

GAOLER. By – by – being what you are!

SOCRATES. You mean – the member of a minority?

GAOLER. Great! The arrow hits! The great philosopher gets it, right in the head! You're a nasty little cult, poisoning the rest of us!

SOCRATES. You know what I call the tyranny imposed on the soul by anger, or fear, or desire, or envy?

The GAOLER *is glaring at him, breathing heavily.*

I call it injustice.

GAOLER. Yeah? I call it dishing out what people like you deserve.

SOCRATES *does not react. For a moment they are looking directly at each other with straight faces.*

Then SOCRATES *smiles.*

SOCRATES. Well, I am truly dished. It seems I was wrong when I told the jury it's easier to avoid death than it is wickedness, because wickedness runs faster. But then, maybe I am about to have a wicked death? (*Inwardly.*) No, for me, I have always thought that, when death comes, it will be a blessing.

The GAOLER *blows a raspberry.*

GAOLER. Don't start the fancy death speech. You're not going to die.

SOCRATES. No? Well, my wife believed Athena wouldn't permit it. But here we are, my execution day!

GAOLER. No way.

SOCRATES. There's a delay? An administrative glitch? Well, at least we're still inefficient, that part of democracy's still with us.

GAOLER. Oh drop it, drop it. You know it's not going to happen.

SOCRATES. Do I?

GAOLER. The games we play with you people – it's fixed!

SOCRATES. Fixed.

GAOLER. In the end it's all fucking political.

SOCRATES. Please explain –

GAOLER. You're going to escape.

A pause.

SOCRATES. I assure you, I am not.

GAOLER. Nah, you've got powerful friends. Course you've got powerful friends! You pose as some kind of rebel, but really you're right in there. Part of it.

SOCRATES. 'It'?

GAOLER. The 'Great It'. The great fix! I mean, no one really wants you dead. Not even that prick Meletus. He just wants the whole Socrates thing well and truly trashed, killing the man could be a bit – y'know. Don't want a smelly old loony like you turning into a hero, do we? So everyone's looking the other way.

SOCRATES. My friends have bribed you?

The GAOLER *shrugs.*

GAOLER. You've got till sunset. If you're still here then, it'll be the – (*Drinking gesture.*)

SOCRATES. Cup.

GAOLER. Right.

SOCRATES. So I'll just walk out – ?

GAOLER. No no, hid in a bale of old prison straw. That's the usual route toffs take out of here.

SOCRATES. Soiled straw for the high and mighty!

GAOLER. Nothing but the best! Cart, straight to Piraeus and a ship.

SOCRATES. Do you approve?

GAOLER. Not for me to say.

SOCRATES. You don't feel your – profession is – well, slighted?

GAOLER. What can I do about it?

SOCRATES. You could give me the poison now.

GAOLER. No no, that has to be at sunset.

SOCRATES. If a thing is to be done, it has to be done properly?

GAOLER. Right.

SOCRATES. It's a ritual.

A pause.

They are looking at each other.

You think I deserve to be put to death.

GAOLER. We've just – got to get back to normal. After all the ructions. Normal, that's all.

SOCRATES. But –

GAOLER. If you go and ask 'What is normal?' I'll – I'll. Yeah. So.

SOCRATES *waits, calmer.*

Cos – no – what I know is, what we're living in't normal. What life should be, we don't need philosophers, judges, tyrants telling us. It's in us, we may hate it, but it is. What life should be.

SOCRATES. You mean the sense of 'right and wrong' is innate within us?

GAOLER. I'm talking about just – living.

SOCRATES. And dying by order of the state, is that 'normal'?

GAOLER. Got to be, hasn't it. If we're going to have justice.

SOCRATES. And how do you feel about taking a bribe to thwart that justice?

The GAOLER *glares – is he going to be violent? But the moment goes and he shrugs.*

GAOLER. The roof of my house needs fixing.

SOCRATES. Ah.

GAOLER. So I need to buy a second slave.

SOCRATES. Ah.

GAOLER. I mean, my wife's been on at me for months to get one.

SOCRATES. Ah.

GAOLER. I mean, she's got the girl, but I need a man –

SOCRATES. Yes.

They look at each other. 'This is how it is.'

A pause.

GAOLER. Right. New straw.

SOCRATES. Is that needed?

GAOLER. Keep up appearances.

SOCRATES. Take a pride?

GAOLER Absolutely. If you don't, what's the point? I'll give the floor a go, too.

As SOCRATES *reflects, the* GAOLER *comes in and out, cleaning. For now he exits.*

SOCRATES (*aside*). Is he right? That it's appearances that matter? That the room be clean, whatever dirty things be done in it? Does a ritual mean nothing in itself, religion mean nothing in itself? Is its power in – the habit? Is all that holds a country together a glue called habit? All that does matter is – that that we kneel together, pray together, chant the same chants, look up to the god-filled sky together, whether Zeus and the whole family are up there on the Olympian clouds or not? Water clock. In my head. Drip drip. Plop plop. My mind plops on. I cannot stop it. Plop.

He laughs.

The GAOLER *enters with new straw. He spreads it on the bed.*

GAOLER. Something funny?

SOCRATES. A plop in my head.

GAOLER. I can brew up some rosemary tea –

SOCRATES. No, not that kind of headache.

The GAOLER *exits.*

(*Aside.*) So – philosophy, 'know thyself', the examined life – does what I teach destroy the glue? Like vinegar, eat into the very thing that holds us together? If you are an enemy of mindlessness, are you an enemy of the state?

A beat.

Plop.

A beat.

Plop.

The GAOLER *enters with a mop and bucket. He begins to mop the floor.*

When you called me an arty-farty thinker –

The GAOLER *sighs and lean on his mop handle.*

– did you mean that I am fooling myself? Am I – caught in a bubble? Is everything I know only – within walls? Like a blown-glass vessel? And – my mind – merely an insect crawling on its inner wall? Bubble of my experience? I have had great experiences, fought in wars, held a comrade in my arms at the Battle of Cunaxa as he screamed into his death, yes, been in the counsels of the great, slept with the great – male, female – but my life, do I pride myself? In my artfulness? Do I merely pride myself in my small circle? Have I grown old? Do the young, Meletus and his fanatical friends – righteous closed minds but do they know something I don't? Are they really the world? While I am in a tiny bubble? For how do we know ourselves? Is the attempt – mere self-justification? Self-aggrandisement? At the very least, smugness? That dangerous feeling that I know what I am, but you, don't? Is this the tool to use, in thinking, doubt, doubt that you are even thinking? So, should I apologise to you? Is Socrates disappearing up his own arse?

A pause.

The GAOLER *is still leaning – all but sagging – on his broom. Then he moves.*

GAOLER. Well. At least you didn't write on the walls, like some.

He exits.

SOCRATES. Meaning – no need to scrub anything of me out, I am already obliterated? Is it all – brutality? For true philosophy, go to the executioners?

A beat.

Plop.

A beat.

Water.

A beat.

Time.

A beat.

Thought.

A beat.

Blood.

Enter the GAOLER.

GAOLER. Your people will be here.

SOCRATES. Yes.

GAOLER. You better get yourself ready. For, y'know –

SOCRATES. My escape.

GAOLER. You're going to be sensible, then.

SOCRATES. Sensible. Meaning – something done with wisdom or prudence, that is likely to be of benefit.

The GAOLER *hesitates, uncertain of that reply, then exits.*

SOCRATES *is still for a moment.*

Then he lies down.

He closes his eyes.

End of Scene Three.

Scene Four: To Phthia

A large cup is on a small tripod table in the centre of the room.

SOCRATES *sleeps. He opens his eyes.*

Strange light.

The DAEMON *appears, masked.*

SOCRATES. What are you?

The DAEMON *is silent.*

I'm dreaming, yes?

The DAEMON *is still silent.*

Do you have something to say to me?

DAEMON. On the third day you will reach Phthia.

SOCRATES. The third day? After what?

DAEMON. On the third day.

SOCRATES. After my escape?

DAEMON. Third day.

SOCRATES. After my execution?

DAEMON. You will reach fertile Phthia.

SOCRATES. Ah. So. Escape, execution, both are death?

DAEMON. Ah my darling, my sweet man, do you want to see me naked?

SOCRATES. Will that make things clearer?

DAEMON. Dreams are always clear.

SOCRATES. But muddy in interpretation.

DAEMON. That's your fault, not mine.

SOCRATES. Are you Asclepius, son of Apollo, patron of poets, god of dreams and healing?

The DAEMON *laughs.*

DAEMON. Oh! High opinion of yourself! Every time you shut your eyes, you think you get a god?

Not laughing.

You know who I am.

SOCRATES. My daemon.

The DAEMON *does not reply.*

A pause.

Why 'fertile' Phthia?

DAEMON. Because it decays.

SOCRATES *looks at the cup.*

At once the light returns to normal.

And ASPASIA *is at the doorway, angry, her back to the cell.*

The DAEMON *retires to a corner, facing the wall, head down, shoulders huddled.*

ASPASIA. No no, I'll talk to him, you all wait there.

SOCRATES. Keeping my friends at bay?

ASPASIA. You can play-act to your cronies later.

SOCRATES. Xanthippe and the boys –

ASPASIA. Out of the city, the boat to Sicily, safe.

SOCRATES. Good. Good.

He closes his eyes and breathes for a moment. Then is chipper again.

And now we are free to get on with the comical-tragical stuff, no? Let Plato in.

ASPASIA. Actually – Plato sent word. He's ill, he can't come.

This is a shock for SOCRATES. *He barely shows it.*

SOCRATES. Oh, he'll be devastated – it's not –

ASPASIA. No, no, he ate something bad, I think –

SOCRATES. I'll send a doctor –

ASPASIA. Don't.

SOCRATES. I must – he wants to be a playwright, silly boy, he neglects himself –

ASPASIA. Actually Plato's not ill.

SOCRATES. Then why –

ASPASIA. I told him to stay away.

The DAEMON *laughs.*

SOCRATES. For what reason?

ASPASIA. I said you didn't want him here.

A beat.

SOCRATES. Why would you do that?

She looks at him.

Ah. Because he'd argue against my escape.

ASPASIA. And you'd listen to him. I've warned you about Plato – you refuse to see the danger in that young man.

SOCRATES. Oh, playwrights are harmless, like all artists they've no idea what they're doing.

ASPASIA. Plato knows. He wants to swallow you whole, you and everything you stand for.

SOCRATES (*laughs*). I don't mind 'being swallowed'. Particularly by a pretty throat.

ASPASIA. Oh spare me – your blindness about beautiful young men –

SOCRATES. Too late to get over that now. No no, maybe it's my fate to be swallowed whole? To live on in the gut of my country's memory, like a slight stomach ache.

ASPASIA. Oh, you'll be celebrated, loved, remembered as the best of us. There are people who will see to that.

SOCRATES. What people?

ASPASIA. People with power. And money. Who think you're too valuable to throw on the fire.

A pause.

SOCRATES. You're talking about Persia.

ASPASIA. Sometimes you can't care who your friends are.

SOCRATES. Even if they're your enemies?

ASPASIA. It doesn't matter what their motive is!

SOCRATES. Even if it's to buy me, buy my country?

ASPASIA. I'm going to save you, by any means possible. Even from yourself.

SOCRATES. Mm. To be saved from one's self. (*A beat.*) So, it's all arranged? Gatekeepers bribed, a disguise at the border – and a new life in exile. Will it be?

ASPASIA. Be what?

SOCRATES. New?

ASPASIA. Of course!

SOCRATES. And where is Persia planning to – deposit me?

ASPASIA. Thessaly.

SOCRATES. Thessaly, ah.

ASPASIA. It'll be symbolic –

SOCRATES. Yes, I see! The site of the clash between the gods and the Titans, my my – highly symbolic.

ASPASIA. You'll be the true Athens in exile.

SOCRATES. Will I have a garden?

ASPASIA. A garden? Yes, well, I – if you want –

SOCRATES. Good. A vegetable patch will be the Agora of this 'true Athens'.

ASPASIA. Socrates –

SOCRATES. A country as a garden. Mmm. Mmm. The citizens of Athens haven't listened to me, maybe the onions of Thessaly will? Bulbous and happy, if a little smelly – growing into happiness, that's what we're all after, no? The human project – happiness? But – the happiness of one can be the sorrow of another, so let us ask –

ASPASIA. Stop it! Stop it! There's no time to spin one of your tangles –

SOCRATES. No no, Aspa my love, my darling, my lover, my collaborator, listen – have we not always agreed that the one thing we must do while alive, is to try to live well?

ASPASIA. All right! All right! Five! I give you five!

ASPASIA *holds up her fist.*

One!

She raises her thumb.

SOCRATES. I haven't made my first point.

ASPASIA. Live well. That was your first point.

SOCRATES. That was the establishment of an assumption, not an argument –

ASPASIA. Don't push it –

SOCRATES. The highest value is to live well, yes?

ASPASIA. Yes yes.

SOCRATES. And we've always agreed, to live well is to live honourably, and justly?

ASPASIA. Yes.

SOCRATES. So is it just for me to get out of here at all, foreign money or not?

She pulls her hand down.

ASPASIA. Just? Is it just for your wife and your sons to be condemned to a social death, widow and orphans of an executed criminal? I don't see anything just in this! Only survival.

SOCRATES. I asked the laws what I should do.

ASPASIA. You asked the laws of Athens –

SOCRATES. Yes, I debated with them.

ASPASIA. Oh really, and what did these grey eminences in your head say?

SOCRATES. That even if one is unjustly treated, one should not return injustice.

ASPASIA. But by escaping you avoid that injustice!

SOCRATES. No, I create another by going against what made me.

ASPASIA. The laws of fucking Athens –

SOCRATES. Yes. They said: we gave you your education. We gave you the freedom you fought the war for. We triumphed against the tyrants when they trampled on democracy. We gave you space to live, to speak.

ASPASIA. And now they are silencing you!

SOCRATES. The laws are all we've got.

ASPASIA. My country, right or wrong?

A long pause.

Then she realises what he is going to do but is too slow to stop him going to the chalice. He drains it and puts it down.

They look at each other.

Then he grins.

SOCRATES. Don't feel a thing.

He looks at his hands, his feet, he shakes his arms.

SOCRATES. Nothing! Maybe it's not a very good year for hemlock.

He laughs.

ASPASIA. You must lie down.

The GAOLER *enters.*

Get him to lie down –

GAOLER. He's –

ASPASIA. Yes – please, can it be undone, an antidote or –

GAOLER (*furious with* SOCRATES). This is completely out of order! What do you think you're doing?

SOCRATES, *a shrug and a smile.*

SOCRATES. Accepting the jury's verdict.

GAOLER. But you're not doing it right! It's not sunset!

SOCRATES. Ah my friend, a true ritualist to the end.

GAOLER. The ritual's buggered, you've seen to that!

SOCRATES. Maybe I've invented a new one.

ASPASIA. Please, please – at least get him to lie down.

DAEMON. She thinks you won't die if you lie down!

GAOLER. We like 'em to walk around at first, work it through the limbs –

SOCRATES, *the gesture of a raised finger at a thought.*

SOCRATES. Yes. The ritual of the impulse. Of the moment. Of true freedom.

ASPASIA (*to the* GAOLER). Can't you –

SOCRATES. 'Live well.' Did I?

Suddenly he is galvanised. He turns away. He is still for a moment then he retches violently, falling on to all-fours.

As the light snaps to strange.

The retching continues. Stops. He wipes his mouth and breathes heavily.

To make manifest – to make public – your life – public – eaten – spewed oh!

He retches.

Am I – am I – am I – a manifesto – for a lost cause? –

Light snapped to normal.

SOCRATES *is gagging.*

ASPASIA. He's –

GAOLER. Get his feet –

ASPASIA. I –

GAOLER. Feet!

The GAOLER *pulls him up behind his arm.*

ASPASIA. He's choking –

GAOLER. Yeah, that does some of 'em in straight away.

ASPASIA. Oh gods –

GAOLER. Just get him flat, on his side.

They lay him on the couch.

That's right, there we go, nice 'n' easy, case I have to tie him down.

ASPASIA. Do what?

GAOLER. It can be best.

ASPASIA. But this is meant to be a civilised poison –

GAOLER. It's fucking hemlock, love –

ASPASIA. No, you just go numb, that's what they say – a democratic death –

GAOLER. Yeah, that's how it's sold. Look – get your friends in here, and steel yourselves.

Light to strange.

SOCRATES *is increasingly desperate, trying to control his thinking.*

SOCRATES. Are you me?

DAEMON. No I'm you.

SOCRATES. I –

DAEMON. Who?

SOCRATES. Me. Where?

DAEMON. You're on your way, darling man.

SOCRATES. The future, what will be thought –

DAEMON. 'I am crossed out in…'

The DAEMON *laughs.*

SOCRATES. I think therefore I am – yes?

DAEMON. Nope.

SOCRATES. The world exists but only as I see it – that it, that it?

DAEMON. Nope.

SOCRATES. But what's – before the thought?

DAEMON. Warmer!

SOCRATES. I almost see it! Catch it! The mind's eye! The flame within we can never know –

DAEMON. Hot!

SOCRATES. Is it – (*Whisper.*) the soul? (*Loud.*) Oh I feel so sick, I –

DAEMON. There is no I –

SOCRATES. But if I cough my lungs up and hold them in my hands, isn't that Socrates?

DAEMON. S'all stuff –

Snap to normal light.

SOCRATES *is in convulsions and retching, the* GAOLER *sprawled across him.*

SOCRATES *is suddenly still. Very carefully, the* GAOLER *withdraws.*

SOCRATES *blinks. He looks at* ASPASIA, *surpised.*

SOCRATES. Where are my friends?

ASPASIA. We're all here.

SOCRATES. Where?

ASPASIA *looks at the* GAOLER, *who shakes his head.*

We need a plan.

ASPASIA. We have one, my darling, your eternal fame –

The DAEMON *laughs.*

SOCRATES. No no! This is what you do. We owe a cock to sacrifice to Asclepius. Pay for it and don't forget.

He turns away and is unconscious.

ASPASIA. Sacrifice to the god of healing? As he dies?

GAOLER. Well – he wants to thank the god, for curing him of life with death. Or maybe it's just a gag.

ASPASIA. Don't you know – don't you have any – of what you, all of you, Athens, have done? You've destroyed a great mind!

GAOLER. Sod great minds. No one's brighter than anyone else.

ASPASIA. You bastards, all of you, you bastards!

She rushes at the GAOLER, *fists raised. He grabs her arms and forces her down.*

A moan from SOCRATES.

ASPASIA *and the* GAOLER *freeze.*

He's still alive.

GAOLER. Hardly, he's paralysed now.

ASPASIA. Can he hear us?

GAOLER. No way of knowing.

ASPASIA. I want to hold him –

GAOLER. No way, the poison'll be in his sweat. (*To the room, i.e. the audience.*) All of you, keep back! Leave this to the specialists.

At once the light snaps to strange.

SOCRATES *laughing.*

SOCRATES. Leave it to the specialists! I argued that once –

DAEMON. Argue is done.

The stage begins to flood with a world of moving leaves, sunlight, distant shining sea.

SOCRATES *turns to the* DAEMON, *who removes the mask.*

SOCRATES. You're my wife.

DAEMON. Only in your head.

SOCRATES. But you won't die –

DAEMON. I will.

SOCRATES. You and the boys, you'll survive –

DAEMON. Widow, widowers, we half die –

SOCRATES. No, you'll be safe in Sicily.

DAEMON. They say in India we burn together.

SOCRATES. That's not rational.

DAEMON. Who said anything is?

SOCRATES. I did?

DAEMON. Why?

SOCRATES. Cos – cos – if we don't know ourselves, there's no hope.

DAEMON. But what about other selves? Did you ever know me?

SOCRATES. Oh get out of my head, go! Live!

DAEMON. I will. But there's a shadow. Of someone not there.

SOCRATES. You are my true love.

The DAEMON, *sarcastic.*

DAEMON. Ho ho ho ho.

The DAEMON *replaces the mask.*

SOCRATES. Love is a daemon.

DAEMON. Yes.

SOCRATES. I argued that too.

DAEMON. Yes.

The stage is now intense with the image of leaves, sunlight and sea. SOCRATES *sits up.*

SOCRATES. Is this Phthia?

DAEMON. You know where it is.

SOCRATES. I –

A blackout.

End of play.

A Nick Hern Book

Cancelling Socrates first published as a paperback original in Great Britain in 2022 by Nick Hern Books Limited, The Glasshouse, 49a Goldhawk Road, London W12 8QP, in association with Jermyn Street Theatre, London

Cover artwork by Ciaran Walsh

Designed and typeset by Nick Hern Books, London
Printed in Great Britain by Mimeo Ltd, Huntingdon, Cambridgeshire PE29 6XX

A CIP catalogue record for this book is available from the British Library

ISBN 978 1 83904 089 4